SO-ADS-669

# UNLEASHING
# THE POWER
## OF
# JOY

# UNLEASHING
# THE POWER
## OF
# JOY

# UNLEASHING THE POWER

## OF

# JOY

HOW TO
RECOGNIZE IT...
GRASP IT...
CLAIM IT...
USE IT!

DALE
CRAWSHAW

© 2001 by
DALE CRAWSHAW

Dale Crawshaw is available for speaking engagements. He can be contacted by e-mail at the following address:

bencrawshaw@hotmail.com

All rights reserved. No part of this book may be reproduced in any form without permission in writing from the publisher, except in the case of brief quotations embodied in critical articles or reviews.

All Scripture quotations, unless otherwise indicated, are taken from the *Holy Bible, New International Version®*. NIV®. Copyright © 1973, 1978, 1984 by International Bible Society. Used by permission of Zondervan Publishing House. All rights reserved.

Scripture quotations marked NASB are taken from the *New American Standard Bible®*, © Copyright The Lockman Foundation 1960, 1962, 1963, 1968, 1971, 1972, 1973, 1975, 1977, 1995. Used by permission.

Scripture quotations marked TLB are taken from *The Living Bible*, copyright © 1971. Used by permission of Tyndale House Publishers, Inc., Wheaton, Illinois 60189. All rights reserved.

Scripture quotations marked NLT are taken from the *Holy Bible, New Living Translation*, copyright © 1996. Used by permission of Tyndale House Publishers, Inc., Wheaton, Illinois 60189, U.S.A. All rights reserved.

Scripture quotations marked AMPLIFIED are taken from *The Amplified Bible* © 1965 Zondervan Publishing House.

Scripture quotations marked PHILLIPS: Reprinted with permission of Scribner, a Division of Simon & Schuster, from The New Testament in Modern English, Revised Edition, translated by J. B. Phillips. Copyright © 1958, 1960, 1972 by J. B. Phillips.

Scripture quotations marked TEV are taken from *Good News Bible: Today's English Version*, 2d ed. Copyright © 1992 by American Bible Society. Used by permission.

Scripture quotations marked KJV are taken from the King James Version.

Library of Congress Cataloging-in-Publication Data

Crawshaw, Dale.
    Unleashing the power of joy : how to recognize it, grasp it, claim it, use it / Dale Crawshaw.
        p. cm.
    ISBN 0-8024-1782-5
    1. Joy—Religious aspects—Christianity. 2. Christian life I. Title.

BV4647.J68 C73 2001
248.4—dc21

                                                                    2001030238

1 3 5 7 9 10 8 6 4 2
Printed in the United States of America

# CONTENTS

# ACKNOWLEDGMENTS

At the church I pastor, we endorse the don't-put-the-preacher-on-a-pedestal philosophy. A minister has specific duties to accomplish, yes, but he's just one of the many parts that make up Christ's body—His church. He needs to minister and be ministered to.

We encourage our entire congregation to be involved in ministry, to find a way to bless everybody they come in contact with, in the community as well as in the church. The people in this special group exude the radiance of Christ so well they have become absolutely contagious in our little corner of the world.

Occasionally, we run ads in the local paper using creative—sometimes off-the-wall—cartoons to let families in the area know of us. They draw folks to visit once. But you know why they come back? People. People who radiate Christ. People contagious with joy!

I'm one of those pastors who absolutely enjoys the ministry. I mean, it's a blast. A big part of my enthusiasm comes from the fact that I'm not bearing the whole load. People who are growing in grace have the joy of the Lord as their strength. They use that strength to bless others and encourage the socks off me.

From children to retirees, our congregation demonstrates how to get the pie out of the sky and eat it. This author is infected with a group of believers' contagious joy, a joy that more and more people can't help but catch.

God bless all of you for your powerful ministry of joy.

# 1

# Get the Pie Out of the Sky and Eat It

*U*ncle Freddie wasn't really my uncle. He claimed to have adopted me, though. He lived next door when I was a kid, just a hundred yards from the Atlantic Ocean in the beautiful Florida Keys. I was his buddy and almost constant companion.

Some nights I'd sleep over at Uncle Freddie and Aunt Flossie's house. He'd hook a huge piece of meat on a heavy-duty rod and reel with a bell attached to the tip of it. Then he'd let the bait drift a couple hundred feet into the dark sea.

When the bell started clanging, it was wake-up time. No matter what hour of the night, Uncle Freddie would rush excitedly to my room and shout, "Sonny Boy, get up. We've got a big one!"

We'd go out and wrestle in a shark that might weigh in at three or four hundred pounds. After we'd brought him in and hoisted him onto the dock, Uncle Freddie would laugh and say, "Isn't it great to be alive, Sonny Boy?"

I don't think there was a day of his life when Uncle Freddie didn't laugh many times. My mom used to play Scrabble with him, sitting next to a big plate glass window that overlooked the ocean. By then, he knew his days were numbered. Leukemia had caught up with him and was relentlessly gaining ground. One day, looking out the picture window, he noticed some buzzards circling over the shoreline, undoubtedly waiting for some dead fish to wash up on the beach. "You won't get me, you buzzards," he hollered, waving his arms and laughing. "I'll skin you before you ever get me. I'm going to live forever."

*God's Holy Spirit is here, so we can taste joy whether we're working or playing, on sunny days or gloomy ones.*

Uncle Freddie never attended church. I don't remember his ever saying much about God. I'm positive if he had known Jesus Christ as his Savior, he would have told me about it.

Years later, when I came to know the Lord, it didn't take me long to observe that a lot of Christians weren't very happy. I couldn't help wondering how someone like Uncle Freddie, who didn't even know the Lord, could be so full of life when many Christians on their way to heaven weren't. He not only had a zest for living when he was in good health, but also when he knew he was soon going to die.

Every time I think of Uncle Freddie, it reminds me that believers ought to be joyful. Often, though, we dwell on the sweet bye-and-bye because we can't cope with the nasty now-and-now.

I've discovered that our pie doesn't have to stay in the sky. It's real. It's edible. God's Holy Spirit is here, so we can taste joy whether we're working or playing, on sunny days or gloomy ones. Even when the whole world caves in right before our eyes.

That brings me to Mike. For several months, I'd been counseling Mike informally over an occasional lunch. He was an enigma to me. He had every reason to be an upbeat guy. He had much to be thankful for. No matter how our conversations started, though, they always ended in the negative. I'd try to steer things in a positive direction, but would rarely succeed. Mike could only see life from the down side.

We were cruising along in conversation one day, discussing something reasonably constructive. Before I had the slightest inkling of how he got there, he found a way to illustrate the subject with the injustice of life. From there, he detailed the inadequacies of humanity and government, not leaving out any of the doomsday stuff. He ended with, "This planet is so full of evil, it's going to self-destruct any day now."

Mike didn't know how to get the pie out of the sky and eat it because he didn't really think there was any pie in the sky in the first place. Joy was a weird, abstract idea to him—Fantasy Island. Life was no joy-factory. It was one big mud fight, and the good guys—like him—were the ones who always got buried in the mud.

"Hey, Mike," I said, "tell me about the last time something happened in your life that was so great you couldn't have planned it that good yourself."

He thought for a while. Finally, he asserted, "I can't remember that ever happening. But—" and he launched into another "everything stinks" rabbit chase.

I tried to change the subject to Atlanta Braves baseball. "They really got creamed last night," he responded.

"They've got to have an off-game once in a while," I came back. "They just got through winning ten in a row!"

"Yeah, but if they don't start hitting, they'll be in big trouble," he predicted with authority.

Mike was addicted to the chemicals of his own negative outlook on life. You're probably not that far gone, but maybe you tend to lean in that direction. If so, it's even more important that you get a grip on the fact that *every* child of God is eligible for joy.

You can begin to reprogram your mind to eliminate all those thoughts about how lousy things are and what a victim you are. Every coin has two sides, including life. Unless you start believing—even grudgingly—that you can grow into a more positive, joyful person, your misery rut will only deepen. Maybe it's time to ask some pointed questions.

Is God almighty, or isn't He?

Is life a temporary journey toward a glorious heaven, or isn't it?

Is the God who knew me in my mother's womb able to work in my mind and heart to bring me joy, or isn't He?

This book offers no magic formulas for happiness. But it will challenge you to believe in the reality of joy—to put things in eternal perspective.

The one who raised the Lord Jesus from the dead will also raise us with Jesus and present us with you in his presence. All this is for your benefit, so that the grace that is reaching more and more people may cause thanksgiving to overflow to the glory of God.

Therefore we do not lose heart. Though outwardly we are wasting away, yet inwardly we are being renewed day by day. For our light and momentary troubles are achieving for us an eternal glory that far outweighs them all. So we fix our eyes not on what is seen, but on what is unseen. For what is seen is temporary, but what is unseen is eternal. (2 Corinthians 4:14–18)

By the way, please take time to read the Scriptures quoted in this book. Your opportunity to grow in joy will be *much greater* if you do.

## INTANGIBLE TANGIBLES

The protective walls of Jerusalem had been torn down. Bandits preyed upon the city at will. Poverty abounded. It's surprising the city existed at all. Talk about a joyless situation!

Nehemiah, a Jewish captive in Persia, held a prestigious position in the opulent kingdom. He sensed a divine urgency to return to his hometown, Jerusalem, with a mission: to rebuild the seemingly unrepairable city walls. With the king's permission and funding, he arrived in Jerusalem to carry out his plan. The citizens welcomed him with open arms, right? Wrong. He was shocked to discover apathy, greed, and disloyalty.

But he refused to be disheartened. He maintained his enthusiasm and faced the impossible by calling on his God, who could do anything. And the God of the impossible proved Himself. In spite of formidable obstacles, those walls were rebuilt in an incredible fifty-two days. Jerusalem was once again a safe place for children to play.

> *If you're expecting life and its toys to make you a consistently joyful person, you're bound for disappointment.*

Joy ran rampant throughout the once-defenseless city. Things were changed for the better. A miracle had occurred before their very eyes! How easy it is to celebrate when things are going great.

"That's what I need to boost my joy," you might be saying. "Something tangible. Something encouraging. Something positive on this earth."

That's logical, but it's not the answer.

If you are alert to what's happening around you, you'll say, "How can I repay the Lord for all his goodness to me?" (Psalm 116:12).

God wants us to count our blessings. He delights in our delight. He enjoys blessing us beyond our wildest dreams. He "richly provides us with everything for our enjoyment" (1 Timothy 6:17).

The tangibles cannot be our primary source of joy, though. If you're expecting life and its toys to make you a consistently joyful person, you're bound for disappointment. To really get a grip on joy, you've got to be two-dimensional. Enjoy the tangibles, yes. I mean, really enjoy them. But don't stop there. Go on to the intangible tangibles—the spiritual side of life. That's where the real joy is. That's where you'll find the fuel for the fire of dynamic living.

In the middle of Jerusalem's celebration, God said, "Go your way, eat the fat, and drink the sweet, and send portions unto them for whom nothing is prepared: for this day is holy unto our Lord: neither be ye sorry; for the *joy of the Lord is your strength*" (Nehemiah 8:10 KJV, italics added).

We're embarking on an adventure to find out how the joy of the Lord gives strength, and not just a little strength, but fuel for fire.

Nothing radiates Christ like joy. Christians used to say they were "on fire" for God. They meant they had an intense desire to serve Him and to affect the lives of others by radiating His life. And they drew others to Him by their manner of living. There is no such thing as a child of God who is "on fire" for Him who lacks joy. Joy is the fuel that turns a spark into a roaring fire. "For you make me glad by your deeds, O LORD; I sing for joy at the works of your hands" (Psalm 92:4)

I started my quest for joy in earnest when I was in my

second year of ministry. I was beginning to get a taste of the fact that the world wasn't waiting with open arms for me to evangelize it. Lots of—or should I say, most of—my ministry dreams were being swallowed by the harsh realities of life.

My wife, Rachel, and I had settled into a small church in a country town just outside of Atlanta. An older woman who attended that church befriended me. As I got to know her, I realized she had experienced a hard life. She'd endured a difficult marriage and many heartaches.

I noticed something very special about Carol, though. She was tuned in to people more than anyone I'd ever met. She was a constant encourager to teens, young career people, and couples. She had a good word for everyone. Her attitude of giving life away in spite of her circumstances made a profound and lasting impact on me. The thought of her still blesses me even these many years later.

Carol's life taught me that joy is not something that surfaces only when things are going well. She had a grip on something genuine. Something stable. Something that worked even when life was just plain stinky. And knowing her convinced me that *anyone* can get a grip on joy. It's not a mystical thing. It's wonderfully possible!

## WHAT A JOY RIDE

Oh, how we get emotionally choked by the circumstances of life. We're usually joyful only when people, places, or things are going our way. But the problem is they go our way only a small percentage of the time.

How about you? Do you struggle to find reasons to be joyful in the routine of life? It's time to dig in and find out what God has to say about being joyful even when life gets 98 percent dull and you feel like you are about to get buried in boredom. Remember, God designed us. And He designed joy. He ought to know how to put the two together!

We're about to take a remarkable journey—an honest-to-goodness joy ride. We're going to consider some of life's difficult questions.

*"How can I learn to live above life's frustrations?"*
*"Is it really possible for me to experience joy?"*
*"Can joy be pushed aside?"*
*"What channels joy to me? What makes it happen in my world?"*
*"Do I go looking for it or does it just show up in my life one day?"*
*"What are the ingredients, the chemistry, of joy?"*
*"How can joy strengthen me?"*
*"Do I have to memorize a certain number of Bible verses to be joyful?"*
*"Can my inherited genes keep me from being joyful? Do I have to have a special personality for it?"*

Let's begin answering those questions by going back to Uncle Freddie. I will never forget the last days of his battle with leukemia. One of the effects of that disease is that the blood pumping through your body feels like molten lava. Your energy level is below zero. It's like coming out of a street-brawl where you were beaten to a pulp. You feel like you're dying, and you are.

There weren't a lot of treatment options back then, and Uncle Freddie knew he wouldn't have many more days to smile at life. I vividly remember one special moment. I didn't know it then, but in less than a month, he'd be gone. We were walking near the ocean and talking about the world around us.

"Hey, Sonny Boy," he said to me, "look at those seagulls. Can you hear those seagulls squawking?"

"Yeah," I said, "I hear 'em."

"I can never hear enough of seagulls squawking," he told me with passion.

We sat down on the dock and dangled our feet in the

warm ocean. "Do you see that ocean? Have you ever seen such beautiful water?"

Living on the Atlantic Ocean was beautiful every day. The smell of salt air, waves capping against the seawall, palm trees swaying. Paradise. But I rarely stopped to appreciate it. Uncle Freddie's love for life made me want to have a smile that wouldn't quit, just like he had.

*Start saturating yourself with what God has to say about Himself and the joy He desires for you.*

"Know what?" he predicted. "We're going to get us some dandy fish today. I just know we're going to catch a couple big-uns." We sat on the dock looking at the blue-green ocean. Silver sparkles dangled from our feet as we splashed them in the salty water. He smiled out loud, "Isn't life just grand, Sonny Boy? It just doesn't get any better than this, does it?"

I was only seven years old, but I remember that conversation word for word. His life made me understand that a human being *can* rise above pain, unfairness, and disappointments. A person can live in a state where nothing can derail his joy-train.

I didn't know—or care—how educated he was. It didn't matter how many important people he knew. He knew joy, and his joy continues to fire me even now.

God is daily loading us with the benefits of this beautiful planet. Are we gleaning the joy contained in it? Do we really want the joy the Lord has for us?

Who wouldn't like to be a consistently joyful person? Are you experiencing it? Is your joy-tank filled up or registering just above empty?

## Abraham Found Joy by Relying on the Supernatural Power of God.

By faith Abraham, when God tested him, offered Isaac as a sacrifice. He who had received the promises was about to sacrifice his one and only son, even though God had said to him, "It is through Isaac that your offspring will be reckoned." Abraham reasoned that God could raise the dead, and figuratively speaking, he did receive Isaac back from death. (*Hebrews 11:17–19*)

**Bible Character Joy Lesson #1**

Try saying, "God, You're just awesome. I belong to You, and I'm going to fellowship with You forever. I'm Your child. You chase me and hunt me down every day just to bless me. You love me with an inexpressible love. You load me with benefits. You're the King of kings. You're the Lord of lords. You're the Alpha and Omega, the Beginning and the End. You're going to create a new heaven and a new earth. I'm going to dwell with You there forever and enjoy it all with You. I'll be Your bride. You have prepared an eternal place for me that won't have one iota of sorrow. Bless Your name!"

Start saturating yourself with what God has to say about Himself and the joy He desires for *you*. "Yet he has not left himself without testimony: He has shown kindness by giving you [earthly blessings] and *fills your hearts with joy*" (Acts 14:17, italics added).

That's the kind of self-talk, or actually God-talk, we need every day. It will bring the joy out of hiding. It'll get the pie out of the sky so we can eat it! And the joyride will be exhilarating.

## BBQ AND THE HIGHWAY PATROL

While you're joyriding, just be sure to watch the speed limit! I was heading toward my dad's house one Sunday afternoon, with the barbecue plate I'd bought for lunch sitting on the seat next to me. My diet won't permit that type of food often, so when I indulge, I really get into it. And, boy, did it smell good.

Without realizing it, I had my old car up to eighty miles an hour, spurred on by the delicious aroma in the air. The highway patrolman headed in the other direction must have smelled it, too. In my rearview mirror, I saw him spin his car around so fast it must have made his head swim.

*Uh-oh,* I thought, *this is going to be an awfully expensive lunch.* I pulled into my dad's driveway, not looking in the mirror but feeling the trooper right behind me. Later, Dad said he almost had a cardiac arrest when he saw the flashing blue lights in his front yard. He recovered quickly, though. He quickly rescued the barbecue and took it to his kitchen before it could be confiscated by the police.

I could see from the look on the patrolman's face that he was a no-nonsense kind of guy, but I tried a little humor anyway. "Preachers shouldn't be going into all the world to preach the gospel that fast, should they, Officer?"

He cracked a tiny smile. "You're a preacher, huh?"

"Yes, sir, and I preached my heart out today, and I was smelling that barbecue and—"

"What'd you preach about?" he interrupted.

"'Trading Troubles for Joy,'" I answered.

"Tell me about it." His smile grew noticeably.

For the next twenty minutes, I shared with him—blue lights flashing all the while—a little bit of what I was learning about joy. Two of our church families drove by, smiling and waving, wishing me Godspeed—though I knew if I'd been going God's intended speed I wouldn't have been in this predicament.

As I finished my roadside sermon, the aroma of my lunch floated out of Dad's kitchen window. I thought, *At $150 minimum for this ticket, that barbecue had better be the best I've ever tasted.*

Officer Martin wasn't through with me, though. He was a Christian, he said, but had been going through some very sad and disappointing times. He shared a couple of heart-wrenching stories. Then he jolted me by saying, "I want my life to be fueled by joy, not bitterness. I'm going to put the things you said to work."

I asked if I might pray with him. And, lights still blinking, we had a wonderful prayer meeting right there by the road. At the end, I was tempted to add, "And, Lord, I claim in Jesus' name that my good brother here is going to give me a warning instead of a ticket." *After all,* I thought, *you have not because you ask not.* But I didn't.

Officer Martin nearly picked me off the ground with a big bear-hug. "The Lord sent you to me today," he said. "I have been so uplifted. Now I'm ready to face my problems with a smile."

He turned to go, then looked back. "And, Preacher." He pointed at me. "Slow down. Next time I'm really going to nail you."

As he drove off with a big grin on his face, I was on cloud nine. I'd almost forgotten the barbecue. Almost.

It turned out to be the best four-dollar barbecue plate I'd ever eaten. I was so high, I devoured it cold, wondering how many more Casey Martins were out there—believers from every walk of life who really wanted to live in the joy of the Lord.

What about you? Want to get the pie out of the nebulous mist and really get into it? Want to go beyond talking about joy to actually experiencing it?

## BIG-PICTURE MENTALITY

For many years, I struggled painfully to find consistent joy. I don't claim to have found all the answers, but those struggles have driven me to seek out the keys to joyful living. And I'm excited to share with you what I've discovered.

God clearly speaks to us through His Word on how, when, where, and why joy is possible in the life of each and every one of His children. We also need to exercise our spiritual senses to taste the joys of life.

I didn't learn these things when everything was going my way. No, I started to understand joy at a time when the bottom had dropped out of my life. I'd lost my business, my home, and even my self-worth. For months, I'd felt like I was being sucked down a whirlpool of misery.

But I sensed a voice inside gently leading me toward the answers. Spiritual hearing is much more acute in times of need.

*"Did you see the stars tonight?"* I heard the Holy Spirit ask in my heart. *"Who created the awe-inspiring universe?"*

"You did, Lord," I said. "You own the cattle on a thousand hills."

*"Then am I not able to meet your every need?"*

Can He or can't He? I thought. It only took me a moment to decide. "Yes, You can, Lord. You keep showing me how awesome You really are."

I listened to the ebb and flow of the crickets' song in the clear night air.

*"What's that, Lord? Did I enjoy the note from my son two weeks ago?"*

"Yes, Lord. People say boys never write notes. They just don't do that kind of thing. That's the only one I've had from him in all the months he's been away at school, and it was very encouraging."

*"Am I what? Am I still savoring it?"*

"Well, yes. I've thought about it several times. In fact, Lord, I really do have a ton of things to be grateful for. Thanks for the reminder."

*"The smile from the cashier?"*

"Funny You should bring that up, Lord. When that cashier smiled at me, it caught me off guard. Not many people smile now-a-days."

*"You say she was one of Your children?"*

"I should've guessed. I was having such a bad day, and that smile jolted me back to a more positive attitude."

*"Am I aware that You place treasures like that in my path every day?"*

"Well, I guess so. But, honestly, Lord, I need to start tuning in better. I do know You plan for me to have joy, and that Your joy will give me all the strength I need."

*"Did I get a blessing from helping my coworker with that problem at work today?"*

"Yeah, Lord, I really did. Wow! I see what You mean. I get the best end of the deal when I reach out to others. But, you know, that feeling doesn't last very long. Whenever I think of my job, Lord, it reminds me that I'm not appreciated there. They are two raises behind what they promised me."

*"Do I know how rich I am compared to most of my brothers and sisters around the world?"*

"Lord, quite honestly, I don't think about that very often."

*"When is the last time I really counted my daily blessings?"*

"I guess it's been a while. OK, Lord, I get the point. You do daily load me with benefits."

*"Do I know I'm co-owner with You of the entire universe?"*

"Well, sure, but it's way beyond my capacity to understand. I am grateful to You, though, and I bless Your holy name."

Did those meditations ever jar me!

I had allowed life to fill my mind with distractions and doubts. I was so preoccupied with upcoming bills that I didn't thank Him for the ones already paid. I'd become so consumed with the big picture that the small blessings were zooming right past me. And with them, the opportunities for joy.

Yep, I still get big-picture mentality sometimes. God has to bounce me around sometimes to get my attention. I have to go through all kinds of highly creative trials and troubles, tough predicaments that are absolutely necessary for my future joy. Nothing teaches patience—which produces spiritual maturity and ultimately joy—better than the school of hard knocks.

*Big-picture mentality always misses the little picture—the taken-for-granted blessings of life, the minute benefits that make each day special.*

De-junking my office, I came across that note my son sent me. It had arrived with a card for my forty-fifth birthday. The card read, "Nothing could ever take the place of having a father like you. Nothing could ever bring the joy that your love does." Then he wrote, "Happy 45th, Dad; but I'll tell everyone else you're still 35; 'cause you can still move like you're 25; and still sometimes act like you're 15. This card and note says it all, Pop. *Hey, we've got lots of beautiful years ahead, and I'm gonna love you more and more through all of them.*"

See why the Lord reminded me of that note? How many blessings like that overwhelm us with joy in a day only to be buried the next by an avalanche of life's pressures?

So, here's my encouragement to you. As you start your journey toward more consistent joy, bank on the fact that God is mistake-free. He will never, ever goof up your life.

And yes, even the really, really difficult things in life are not missed opportunities for God's plan for you. They are His plan for you.

This doesn't mean, of course, that we have only a hope of future joys—we can be full of joy here and now even in our trials and troubles. [Taken in the right spirit,] these very things will give us patient endurance; this in turn will develop a mature character, and a character of this sort produces a steady hope, a hope that will never disappoint us. (Romans 5:3–5 PHILLIPS)

You are in big trouble if you're always pushing and tugging, trying to get life to go the way you think it ought to. Demanding life to be a certain way is impossible! Big-picture mentality always misses the little picture—the taken-for-granted blessings of life, the minute benefits that make each day special. The big picture isn't going to be painted today. It's a process. You won't see a hundredth of why today came out the way it did until you set foot in heavenly New Jerusalem.

Do you want to consistently taste the goodness of life? If you do, you're going to have to taste it in small bites—in the sweetness of little things. In the delicate beauty of once-camouflaged pleasures.

So get tuned in. Ask God to help you perceive the hundreds of divine benefits you've gotten in the habit of over-looking.

### Nebuchadnezzar Forfeited Joy when Pride Ruled His Heart.

The king reflected and said, "Is this not Babylon the great, which I myself have built as a royal residence by the might of my power and for the glory of my majesty?" . . . Immediately the word concerning Nebuchadnezzar was fulfilled, and he was driven away from mankind and began eating grass like cattle. . . his hair [grew] like eagles' feathers and his nails like birds' claws. . . [After a season, he came to his right mind and said,] "Now I, Nebuchadnezzar, praise, exalt and honor the King of heaven, for all His works are true and His ways just, and He is able to humble those who walk in pride." *(Daniel 4:30, 33, 37 NASB)*

**Bible Character Joy Lesson #2**

## DR. BUBBA

As a college student in south Florida, I was knocking on doors at an apartment complex late one afternoon, sharing Christ with anyone who would even half-listen. A very handsome and personable fellow answered my rap at one door. I soon learned he was a second-year medical student visiting his fiancée. He went by the nickname Bubba. That seemed an odd name for a guy not far from becoming a physician. I could just imagine someone saying, "Dr. Bubba, I've been feeling just awful lately. What do you think it is, Dr. Bubba?"

I began to share God's awesome plan of salvation. He became increasingly inquisitive about what the Bible had to say about eternal life and other issues. He seemed determined to understand this new concept.

We had many marathon conversations. For the next four days, we were together almost night and day. He asked every question I could imagine and some I couldn't. When I left him, I'd go back to my dorm and stay up half the night looking up the answers. The next day, exhausted but running on adrenaline, I'd tell him what I'd discovered.

Late one afternoon, he said, "I've done enough talking. I want to ask Christ to be my personal Savior."

The moment Bubba trusted Christ, the change in his countenance and outlook astounded his family, friends, and fellow medical students. He was not even close to the same person they had known. In fact, his fiancée found herself engaged to a whole new man.

"I never knew this kind of joy was possible," Bubba said weeks later. "I can't believe I've missed out on it all these years."

I lost contact with Bubba after a few months. At that time, he was a growing Christian destined to have a marked influence for Christ in his community. The joy he had to share was absolutely irresistible.

Sharing your joy with someone who needs it is a real joy-builder in itself. Don't miss the chance. The only joy greater than telling someone the good news of the eternal salvation Christ has bought and paid for in full is watching the joy in action after someone has accepted Him.

So get the pie out of the sky and eat it. You're about to see that it's yours for the enjoying. Not just now and then, but every day.

# 2

# Out of This World

Clinton Clickner is one of my favorite people. About ten years ago, Clinton was driving home from work. Suddenly, he saw two cars racing toward him, one of them in his lane. It struck him head-on doing at least ninety miles per hour. That made it a 140 mph collision.

Incredibly, Clinton survived, but he slipped into a coma. While he lay as still as death in intensive care, I stood beside his bed remembering that ever-present twinkle in his eye. Clinton had the uncanny gift of always finding something to laugh about. He recognized the humorous side to almost everything. But this? If he ever regained consciousness, I wondered, would he still be able to laugh?

I'll never forget the day he woke up from that three-month coma. When I walked into his hospital room, the first thing he said was, "I'm too used to fun for this kind of stuff." Then he laughed and made some joke about living longer because he'd gotten all that extra sleep.

His body sustained numerous lifelong complications

from that accident. The next ten years were a continual
near-death struggle for him. The amazing thing, though, is
that he never lost his joy. "I can't wait to get to heaven," he
told me not long ago, "because I want to see God smile, and
I want to smile back."

People like Clinton assure me that joy is not a rare commodity God gives to just a select few. Nor is it only attain-
able when life's circumstances smile on us.

I have times when I allow nasty weeds of indifference to
grow in my heart. On those occasions, one look at my
countenance says it all. *Throw this day straight out the door, buddy.*
*Maybe next week—or next month—will be better.*

Even in low times like that, God is engineering special
opportunities to give me joy. That's hard to believe when
I'm going through the mill, but it's absolutely true.

> *The Father, the Son, and the Holy Spirit*
> *are chasing you down to bless you, to*
> triply *see to it that you don't go*
> *through life joyless.*

I don't deserve it. At times like that, I'm not even looking
for it. Nonetheless, God wants me to taste His joy.

*The Holy Spirit gives us joy.* Paul wrote to the Thessalonian
believers concerning this joy:

> For we know, brothers loved by God, that he has
> chosen you, because our gospel came to you not simply
> with words, but also with power, with the Holy Spirit
> and with deep conviction. You know how we lived
> among you for your sake. You became imitators of us
> and of the Lord; in spite of severe suffering, you wel-
> comed the message with the joy *given by the Holy Spirit.*
> (1 Thessalonians 1:4–6, italics added)

*The Lord Jesus gives us joy.* Some of Christ's final words to His disciples were promises of joy. His desire for them—as for you and me today—is this: "I am coming to you [the Father] now, but I say these things while I am still in the world, so that they may have *the full measure of my joy* within them" (John 17:13, italics added).

*Our heavenly Father gives us joy.* We have dozens of promises from God the Father concerning His commitment to fill us with joy. Many of them are connected to His unfathomable love for us. This is one of those promises: "Satisfy us in the morning with your unfailing love, that we may *sing for joy and be glad all our days*" (Psalm 90:14, italics added).

Did you get that? Brace yourself. The Godhead is after you! The Father, the Son, and the Holy Spirit are chasing you down to bless you, to *triply* see to it that you don't go through life joyless. Isn't that incredible? What a good reason to celebrate.

## I RECKON IT SO

I'd like you to consider these life-changing truths:

*In Christ you are spiritually alive!* Christ arose from the dead. When God looks at you, He sees you *clothed in the righteousness of Christ!*

*In Christ you have a home waiting for you in heaven!* And He's coming *in person* to take you there.

*In Christ you have supernatural gifts!* Take a moment to look at the appendix. Take in—or try to take in—the gifts God bestowed on you when you were born into His family through Christ. You'll see why I believe *you are a spiritual zillionaire.*

Set your sights not on things down here but on the rich treasures and joys of heaven. Heaven, your future home. Heaven, where Jesus sits in the place of honor and power. Let heaven fill your thoughts. Don't spend your time worrying about the details down here.

When I was in the home-building business, my partner supervised the physical construction responsibilities while I handled the business and sales end of things. When we discussed how we would build a house, I might say, "This is how I visualize it. I think you should do that part first, and then we'll do the next phase this way."

He wasn't afraid to disagree with me. He'd been in the business a long time and had a mind of his own. But once we came to an agreement, he'd always say, "I reckon it so." He was a country boy, and that's how he'd talk. Whenever he reckoned it so, I could always count on it. He did exactly as he promised.

You know what we ought to say about the fact that God is plotting to inject us with joy? *"I reckon it so. I'm counting on it!"*

You might have the uglies big time. You may want to just tell the world how miserable your life is. Maybe you've got such scary problems or heartaches that you don't even want to be anywhere near yourself!

During those yucky times, say by faith, "I reckon it so that You are more than able to do what I absolutely cannot do for myself. I'm surely not going to be able to manufacture any joy with this lousy attitude. But I'm going to appropriate by faith what I don't feel. I'm going to latch on to the spirit of joy until people stare at me, dumbfounded, and say, 'What in the world happened to you?'"

Even your heart—described in Scripture as the seat of your emotional being—can pump joy into you. How you view life and your problems can give you amazing doses of joy. Anticipate victory, not defeat. Anticipate joy, not sorrow.

Say to yourself, *God is good. Life is good. My life is good. I am going to walk in joy!* Get a grip on promises like this one: "Though you have not seen him, you love him; and even though you do not see him now, you believe in him and are *filled with an inexpressible and glorious joy,* for you are receiving the goal of your faith, the salvation of your souls" (1 Peter 1:8–9, italics added).

Remember, joy comes directly from God. I'm in God's family. I am personally related to Him. I have joy because of who I am in Christ.

But further still, I get joy from God simply because He *decided* to *give* it to me. Scripture promises that. Because God the Father, God the Son, and God the Holy Spirit are all givers of joy. In other words, I can't lose if I just stay in the game. If I just work at moving toward the goal, He will provide the power and encouragement I need to get there.

Let's take a further look at how to get the pie out of the sky and start tasting it. The following factors contribute to joyful living: (1) how I view life; (2) the supernatural benefits of being God's child; (3) the chemistry of joy; and (4) sharpening my spiritual senses.

## HOW I VIEW LIFE

Am I a pessimist? Am I negative? Do I fail to appreciate the little things in life?

If I have fine-tuned my ability to discover the negative side of everything and everyone, I'm in big trouble. Like my friend Mike, who ran on the adrenaline of his custom-designed "It's only going to get worse" attitude. Mike spent so much of his time imagining how everything could go wrong that he had no energy left to perceive the many things that went right!

*Smiles and genuine love are almost impossible to argue with.*

I can learn to experience joy consistently by looking at life as a special, wonderful gift from God. As His child, I am uniquely and unconditionally loved by Him. I can bank on that fact every minute of every day that I draw breath on this planet.

> And I pray that you, being rooted and established in love, may have power, together with all the saints, to grasp how wide and long and high and deep is the love of Christ, and to know this love that surpasses knowledge—that you may be filled to the measure of all the fullness of God. (Ephesians 3:17–19)

## BECAUSE I'M GOD'S CHILD

Linda half-listened as she stared out a large window at the tall south Florida palms. She was a beautiful young woman and a college cheerleader; she was all that girls often long to be. Yet a faint smile barely masked her sad heart. She had been abused as a child, and the pain had driven her into the drug scene.

She seemed to be in a daze as I shared with her the message of eternal life through the person of Jesus Christ. "Maybe God is there," she sighed, "but where was He when my daddy was hurting me?"

This was the third time we had talked. I had hoped that my college classmates and I could have a healing effect on her damaged emotions. Smiles and genuine love are almost impossible to argue with. Still, the emptiness in her eyes revealed how desperately Linda needed to know God. We were at a stalemate.

Then I noticed the window she'd been staring through begin to fog up with late afternoon mist. "That glass was clear a moment ago, wasn't it?" I said. "You felt as if you were sitting outside, didn't you?"

"Yeah," she answered half-heartedly.

I continued. "That mist revealed the glass, didn't it?"

Another "Yeah."

"Now you know there's a window there for sure, don't you?"

A third "Yeah."

"Linda," I pleaded, "God has been using the power of His Word, the power of His Spirit and the power of love to reveal Himself to you. The evidence is adding up just like the mist is sticking to that clear pane of glass."

For the longest time, she said nothing. Then, for the fourth time, she said, "Yeah." But this one was different. A light seemed to come on in her head. "He is real, isn't He?" she said. "And He does love me, doesn't He?"

Moments later, Linda prayed to receive Christ. And let me tell you, she was one transformed young lady. Joy simply took over her heart and started overflowing to everyone she got within sight of. The intangible had become tangible. A personal relationship between her and God was supernaturally born. Previously hollow eyes glowed.

Royalty became a reality in Linda's life. She was a child of the King now, and her new countenance spoke volumes. Get this: "Therefore, since we have been justified through faith, we have peace with God through our Lord Jesus Christ, through whom we have gained access by faith into this grace in which we now stand. And we rejoice in the hope of the glory of God" (Romans 5:1–2).

## Mary Found Joy by Wholeheartedly Believing the Word of the Lord.

"But why am I so favored, that the mother of my Lord should come to me? As soon as the sound of your greeting reached my ears, the baby in my womb leaped for joy. Blessed is she who has believed that what the Lord has said to her will be accomplished!"

And Mary said: "My soul glorifies the Lord and my spirit rejoices in God my Savior, for he has been mindful of the humble state of his servant. From now on all generations will call me blessed, for the Mighty One has done great things for me—holy is his name." (Luke 1:43–49)

**Bible Character Joy Lesson #3**

Perhaps you already know God as Linda came to know Him, but you're not consistently tasting the joy He offers. It's time to stop staring out the window of life wishing and wondering about it. Joy is real, and it's a gift that God makes available to each and every one of His children. It's yours. And just like the manna God provided for Israel, the supply is unlimited!

So God the Father, God the Son, and God the Holy Spirit are working at filling my heart with joy. Just think, *one of the actions of Almighty God is to bestow joy on little ol' me!*

## THE CHEMISTRY OF JOY

I'll never forget my high school chemistry teacher, Doc Pendergas. Doc had worked in an insane asylum before he became a teacher. Honestly. I think he brought some insanity with him to school. He was one interesting character!

He had a formidable challenge in teaching me chemistry. I just didn't get it. This, mixed with that, in this equation, equals something or other. More than once, my mixtures caused small explosions in our school lab. My classmates would fight not to be my lab partner out of fear of bodily injury!

Every so often, I actually understood something. That was no small miracle.

Understanding the chemistry of joy is often like high school chemistry—baffling. We just don't get it. We know it works, but we can't seem to make it work in our own lives. It says in Hebrews 5:11–12, "We have much to say about this, but it is hard to explain because you are slow to learn. In fact, though by this time you ought to be teachers, you need someone to teach you the elementary truths of God's word."

*You just don't get it, do you, Dale? You ought to be more spiritually consistent by now. You ought to be mature.* "Anyone who lives on milk, being still an infant, is not acquainted with the teaching about righteousness. But solid food is for the mature, who by constant use have trained themselves to distinguish good from evil" (Hebrews 5:13–14).

*As we grow spiritually, we learn to sense the sharks and barracudas of life lurking in the shadows just waiting to devour our joy.*

Biblically speaking, *solid food* means deep truths that can help us become spiritually mature. Babies must move from a

diet of strictly milk to vegetables and proteins for their muscles and bones to grow in size and strength. They don't become proficient in the skills needed for adulthood until they
move from milk to meat! The same is true in a spiritual
sense. Ingesting God's Word gives us strength to rise above
the pressures of life that would otherwise squelch our joy.

## SHARPENING MY SPIRITUAL SENSES

Active *spiritual* senses are necessary for us to understand
joy. It's time to sharpen and to rely on our spiritual senses,
not our physical senses, to tell us what's going on around us.
To respond scripturally to things that steal our joy and to
embrace things that heap joy upon us!

> I keep asking that the God of our Lord Jesus Christ,
> the glorious Father, may give you the Spirit of wisdom
> and revelation, so that you may know him better. I pray
> also that the eyes of your heart may be enlightened in
> order that you may know the hope to which he has
> called you, the riches of his glorious inheritance in the
> saints, and his incomparably great power for us who be-
> lieve. (Ephesians 1:17–19)

Don't think your senses can't be sharpened. I remember
times I was scuba diving in the Keys with a shark cruising
the depths nearby. The shark might have been on the other
side of the reef, well beyond visibility underwater. Yet, I
knew it was there. How did I feel the shark's presence? I'm
not sure, but I did!

More than once I sensed something following me. I'd
turn around and there would be a huge barracuda grinning
at me with a mouthful of razor sharp teeth. Near a reef
where I often dove, one barracuda stalked me so often I
gave him a name, Cody—Cody the Cuda.

I believe as we grow spiritually, we learn to sense the sharks and barracudas of life lurking in the shadows just waiting to devour our joy. We can also learn the attitudes and actions that allow our joy to rise to the surface. Physical challenges don't hinder the spiritual senses. In fact, physical limitations can help to sharpen them.

After speaking in a Los Angeles church, I met with another group in a conference room. As we got ready to begin the session, I noticed a wheelchair at the side door. A fourteen-year-old girl laboriously guided herself right to the front. Though her body was twisted and deformed and her face disfigured, her bright eyes revealed well-tuned mental faculties.

As I spoke, she listened eagerly. It became evident to me that she loved to hear God's Word taught. The countenance of that girl strapped in a wheelchair was absolutely radiant.

During the long flight back to Atlanta, I couldn't get that little lady off my mind. If the joy of the Lord could give her the strength to reflect Christ, I was without excuse. She'd found a way to tap into something beyond her circumstances. Her joy was real. It was supernatural. In spite of extreme physical limitations, her spiritual senses were razor-sharp. The joy she exuded wasn't based on things going her way.

With some physical limitations of my own—I've lost two-thirds of my kidney function and half my hearing—I understand a little about how it feels to be physically challenged. God sometimes brings a person like that into my life when I'm feeling sorry for myself.

Recently I said to a friend, "Heard you didn't have a good week."

"That's true in one respect," he responded, "but I kept asking God to help me focus on the fact that He's *daily* loading me with blessings. Normally I wouldn't have seen them. Usually I would have been totally bummed out. But I began to think about things from a spiritual perspective, and my disposition brightened dramatically."

That's exercising spiritual senses! How things are going *does not* determine the availability of joy. That's not part of the chemistry. We must focus way beyond the highs and lows of this flimsy life to find true contentment.

Joy. Don't you wish we could bottle it? Like catching fireflies and putting them in a jar? Gather happy feelings, bottle them, and say, "See! I have joy. It's visible. It makes me glow."

We want experiencing joy to be just that simple. It's going to be very elusive, however, unless we *regularly exercise* our spiritual senses. When we do, and the spirit man grows stronger, something invisible yet very real rises within us—joy. Joy that turns the blahs into the hallelujahs.

Do you believe joy is possible in your life? Do you reckon it so? Believing is seeing, and it's time to start believing.

# 3

# Dry Out the Firewood

*T*orture. That's what it was, just plain torture. A rare Atlanta blizzard. Followed by an ice storm. Followed by a
week of subfreezing temperature. Winter's fury come south.
The power had been out for days. Several of our neighbors decided to bundle up and beat the cold by playing in
the white stuff. *Well, why not?* I thought. *Mr. Winter, you can't
get me. See, I'm out here right in the middle of your onslaught having a
wonderful time!*
My Florida blood absolutely refused to cooperate with
that nonsense. The whole time I was out, it screamed at me.
*If you don't get me warm, I'm going on strike. I'll stop flowing through
these cold veins and arteries and turn you into a human ice cube!*
So I succumbed and returned to the house. An outdoors-
man I was not. I'd seldom attempted to build a fire in our
basement fireplace. I did have some wood, though it was totally saturated with frozen moisture. I tried everything to
dry it out, but it was just plain waterlogged.

*Just like wet wood, a disposition dampened*
*by a selfish spirit won't radiate joy.*

In desperation, I built a box-like contraption to hold a couple dozen pieces of wood and placed the wood-filled box in a sunny spot in the backyard. Every hour or so, I tilted my drying box to the exact angle of the sun. In spite of the cold air, the bright sunshine began to dry out that firewood. And this Florida boy was more than willing to spend much of the night making sure the roaring fire never died down.

Just like wet wood, a disposition dampened by a selfish spirit won't radiate joy. The fire of joy will only burn brightly when we take the necessary steps to dry out our firewood—to search our hearts and be sure our wants are not dampening and quenching God's Spirit within us.

Here is God's game plan to make sure His Spirit has the freedom to burn brightly in our fireplace.

> Do not let any unwholesome talk come out of your mouths, but only what is helpful for building others up according to their needs, that it may benefit those who listen. And do not grieve the Holy Spirit of God, with whom you were sealed for the day of redemption. Get rid of all bitterness, rage and anger, brawling and slander, along with every form of malice. Be kind and compassionate to one another, forgiving each other, just as in Christ God forgave you. (Ephesians 4:29–32)

While I served as an associate pastor in a growing young church, I found out just how powerful a joyful spirit could be.

I was called upon to preach occasionally, and though I

wasn't a dynamic speaker, I really did want to be a blessing to the listeners.

Just as a pessimist can lower the spiritual temperature of a room, a joyful person can fire it up. Pam was that kind of person. If she had been the only person in the audience, she would have heard an inspired sermon from me.

Her smile radiated. Her eyes glowed. Her attentiveness soared with every word. Her joyful heart could take a so-so sermon and turn it into something dynamic. When she was in the audience, I had the feeling that I'd really nailed it. Her uplifting spirit told me that every bit of sacrifice, every ounce of energy I put into ministry was fruitful.

Pam didn't have a trouble-free life, either. Among other challenges, she was battling cancer.

"You're such a joy bringer," I once told her. "I can feel your smile even over the phone."

"Thank you for telling me that," she responded. "Your encouragement will help me with the struggles ahead."

## HAWAII OR BUST

Gene was as opposite from Pam as night from day.

He'd lost his job. An injured back kept him from finding another one. Most of his self-esteem had slipped away, and it appeared the bank would soon foreclose on his home.

He was a fellow Christian in trouble, and I sensed God's leading to come alongside him during that low time in his life. To help save his home from foreclosure, I agreed to buy a couple of lots he owned. I paid him a large down payment, and as time went on, I chipped away at the balance until it was less than a thousand dollars. The final payment was not due for several weeks.

Gene called me one night. "My Sunday school class is going to Hawaii," he said, "and I need seven hundred dollars more to go."

"I've been paying you regularly, Gene, as I agreed," I answered. "With my business collapsing, I can barely feed my family. There's no way I can pay you seven hundred dollars right now."

I couldn't believe what happened next. That six-foot-four, two-hundred-fifty pound man began to cry like a baby. I mean, he had a major misery attack. "So I'm not going to Hawaii because you won't pay me my money," he wailed, and carried on for several minutes.

After I hung up, I thought, *Is this the best we can do as God's children? Bawling because he can't go to Hawaii on the money of a brother who is about to lose his shirt?*

> *The people I've known who are the most*
> *unhappy are those who are the*
> *most self-centered.*

Do you see the difference between Pam's attitude and Gene's? Pam had an others-first philosophy of life. Gene acted cordially only as long as it benefited himself. In hard times, Pam's response and Gene's were totally opposite. Troubles squeezed joy out of Pam whereas they brought the uglies out of Gene.

Pam placed the needs of others before her own. She made it a habit to soak in the Sonlight of God's love and refused to be smothered by *I, me,* and *my.* What did she get in return? Joy! A joy worth far more than anything she sacrificed to put God and others first.

The people I've known who are the most unhappy are those who are the most self-centered. Self-consumed people spend an enormous amount of energy trying to live by how they feel at the moment. They try, and usually fail, to manipulate things to work out as they want them to.

I'll tell you, they've got the chemistry all backward—

and remember, I'm an authority on chemistry gone wrong. God's formulas always work if we follow them. When we choose to yield to the directions of God's Holy Spirit, good things happen in our lives.

> But the fruit of the Spirit is love, joy, peace, patience, kindness, goodness, faithfulness, gentleness and self-control. Against such things there is no law. . . .
> . . . Let us not become weary in doing good, for at the proper time we will reap a harvest if we do not give up. Therefore, as we have opportunity, let us do good to all people, especially to those who belong to the family of believers. (Galatians 5:22–23; 6:9–10)

Joy won't come through getting. If you want to experience the fullness of life, you have to think backward from the me-first philosophy that surrounds us. If your life is all about getting, you need a new lifestyle—a giving one.

The bottom line is, you have to give to really live! The only way you are going to have a full heart, the only way you're going to consistently taste joy, is for the kingdom to matter more to you than *you* matter to you. "Give to others, and God will give to you. Indeed, you will receive a full measure, a generous helping, poured into your hands—all that you can hold. The measure you use for others is the one that God will use for you" (Luke 6:38 TEV, italics added).

---

## Ruth Found Joy and Blessings by Putting Others First.

Boaz replied, "I've been told all about what you have done for your mother-in-law since the death of your husband. . . . May the LORD repay you for what you have done. May you be richly rewarded by the LORD, the God of Israel, under whose wings you have come to take refuge."

. . . The women said to Naomi: "Praise be to the LORD, who this day has not left you without a kinsman-redeemer. May he become famous throughout Israel! He will renew your life and sustain  you in your old age. For your daughter-in-law, who loves you and who is better to you than seven sons, has given him birth." (Ruth 2:11–12; 4:14–15)

**Bible Character Joy Lesson #4**

---

## STONE CLOUD NINE

It was a muggy, overcast day. Storm clouds stalked the horizon as I surveyed Georgia's beautiful Lake Lanier. Stones of all shapes and sizes lined the shore.

I love to skip stones. The farther they skip across the water, the more I jump up and down like a little kid. Maybe you don't enjoy anything as carefree as stone-skipping. If not, I hope you have something as much fun to smile about. Life's little pleasures should not be missed.

Oblivious to the deteriorating weather, I picked up some good skippers and started tossing. Some of them were real winners. I was having a banner day. One of those stones skipped all the way to the opposite shoreline.

Now, before you call me Superarm, I'll admit the other side wasn't quite the length of a football field away. But that was still more than twenty stone-skips. Whoop-ee! Wowie, zowie! I was on stone cloud nine.

At dinner, when I proudly told my teenaged kids that I'd set a new American—and probably world—record for stone-skipping, they rolled their eyes and said, "Sure you did, Dad."

Regardless, it was a special day for me because a picture lesson about life and how to live it victoriously had come to me.

The lake represents the *hassles of life* with their negative emotional pull. The storm clouds are *the stuff that frightens us*—problems, worries, criticisms, insecurities. The shoreline from which I launched the stones is *this very moment*. And the opposite shoreline is *the end of whatever day I'm living in.* Not yesterday. Not tomorrow. Today. Each stone's trip across the lake represents *the spiritual and emotional journey across today*—the one and only chance at living, since tomorrow does not yet exist.

The negative pull of life is ready and waiting to swallow me up, just as that lake is after each stone, silently waiting to engulf it and suck it all the way to the murky bottom.

The stones I've skipped, or tried to, illustrate the joy-potential of different Christian lifestyles and dispositions.

## Mr. Big Stuff

I'll call the first one Mr. Big Stuff. This stone is rough edged and bulky. "Don't try to tell me how to live," boasts Mr. Big Stuff. "That's the way my daddy and my granddaddy churched, and I guess it's good enough for me." He's living on inherited genes and traditions. No Bible reading. No quality fellowship. No men's retreats. It's go to work, come home, watch TV, and repeat. Cut the grass on Saturday, and endure another sermon on Sunday. He may look substantial, but a hassle comes along and he's down for the count. No skipping for this stone. The first contact with resistance, and it's sink-city.

## Ms. Glory Hallelujah

Next comes Ms. Glory Hallelujah, a paper-thin stone. "Pr-raise the Lord. Isn't Jesus good?" exclaims this Christian. She looks and acts on fire for God, but she's mostly running on adrenaline. Serious thinking, reading Christian books, or home Bible study? Are you kidding? She's too wired, too busy with every imaginable hyperactivity. Ms. Glory Hallelujah is pretty thin when it comes to substance. Oh, she hits the water beautifully, but then she sails too high into the air, quickly turning sideways. That's trouble. Getting high without any depth means a quick plunge straight down.

## Mrs. Ain't Life Good

For Mrs. Ain't Life Good, life really is good. This stone *looks* good but is a little too thick to skip. And life's not all about her and her blessings. She has some spiritual symmetry. Some depth. But it's mostly in theory. Mrs. Ain't Life Good gives God the credit for her blessings, yet she's consumed with her career, her ambitions, her possessions, and even her own religious importance. She's good for three, four, five, six, maybe even seven skips! But that extra weight is just too much to overcome. Once something goes drastically against all of her good vibrations, it's a trip to the bottom.

## Dr. Did It My Way

Dr. Did It My Way is an interesting sort, shaped more square than oval. He's up one day and down the next. Why? The rough edges just won't budge. There's church attendance. There's Bible reading. There's commitment to the Lord's work. But don't dare rub against a pride point. "When I said that's just the way I am, I meant it!" Some days, Dr. Did It My Way will skip and skip and skip—jump right over those problems with a smile. Other days are a disaster. It takes just one of those really blunt edges to meet the water a certain way, and it's head-over-heels pandemonium, then ker-plunk.

You might see yourself in one of these four stones. Don't despair. There are enough scriptural principles in this book, and tons more for you to uncover on your own, to radically change your disposition and your life.

Actually, you're not a lifeless stone but a living soul. No matter how deep the scars and blemishes are on you, your God is able—fully able—to build within you a life of hope and joy.

## Mr. Contentment

Our last stone, Mr. Contentment, has been through wind and storms and intense heat just like the others. His rough edges have been worn smooth. The big difference is in how he's responded to the elements of life. Instead of becoming prideful, self-righteous, self-absorbed, or bitter, he became better. Don't expect perfection. There are some scars, bumps, and bruises. But Mr. Contentment is mostly oblivious to all of that. He knows that skipping to the other shore without getting swallowed up by that cold, forbidding lake is an exhilarating experience.

Mr. Contentment is the Christian we all can be. The time can come in our lives when we look toward each day's end *knowing* our happy, steadfast spirit is going to propel us over every negative circumstance that comes our way.

That's living. That's a taste of heaven. That's getting the pie out of the sky and devouring it.

Salvation comes by faith, but Christian victory—that is, learning to skip over today's hassles—comes through obedience to God's Word. Obedience always brings a special measure of joy.

What if you don't want to be obedient to God's Word? It's an even more exhilarating joy when you obey at those times when you simply don't want to. That makes you strong. You experience—you taste—a joy you never imagined possible. Remember, the more demanding the act of obedience, the greater the joy!

Jesus said, "If you obey my commands, you will remain in my love, just as I have obeyed my Father's commands and remain in his love. I have told you this so that my joy may be in you and that your joy may be complete" (John 15:10–11).

*He longs for you to be in His family.*
*Heaven celebrates every time one*
*person comes to Christ.*

### SUPERNATURALLY BORN

If we who know Christ need to work at how to really enjoy life, how much more in despair of joy is someone who doesn't know Him?

Once a person receives Christ as his personal Savior, he is supernaturally reborn. He is indwelt by God's mighty Spirit. He gets a whole new motivation and power source for living. He instantly inherits the capacity to start experiencing true joy and happiness.

"I tell you the truth, whoever hears my word and believes him who sent me has eternal life and will not be condemned; he has crossed over from death to life." (John 5:24)

This righteousness from God comes through faith in Jesus Christ to all who believe. There is no difference, for all have sinned and fall short of the glory of God, and are justified freely by his grace through the redemption that came by Christ Jesus. (Romans 3:22–24)

For it is by grace you have been saved, through faith—and this not from yourselves, it is the gift of God—not by works, so that no one can boast. (Ephesians 2:8–9)

Have you ever personally asked Jesus Christ to be your Savior? If not, there is no better time to do so than this very moment. He longs for you to be in His family. Heaven celebrates every time one person comes to Christ. "I tell you that in the same way there will be more rejoicing in heaven over one sinner who repents than over ninety-nine righteous persons who do not need to repent" (Luke 15:7).

## REKINDLING THE JOY OF SALVATION

How I remember the day I trusted Christ as my Savior! I bubbled over with joy for months. I wanted to share my experience with anyone who would listen. I was so excited about my newfound faith I even went to nursing homes, where folks often went to sleep while I was talking. That didn't faze me one bit. I figured hearing the truth in their sleep was better than not hearing it at all.

It's a sad thing, though, when that initial joy begins to wear off. We kind of slip into neutral, or even into reverse. We reason, "I'm doing the best I can. I go to church and read my Bible some. I don't guess I can expect God to really change my disposition. This is the way I am, and I'll probably always be this way."

No, you won't! Once you're born into God's family, you are forever His child. He takes a personal, tireless interest in helping you become spiritually prosperous.

---

### The Rich Young Ruler Forfeited Joy by Worshiping Security

Jesus answered, "If you want to be perfect, go, sell your possessions and give to the poor, and you will have treasure in heaven. Then come, follow me."

When the young man heard this, he went away sad, because he had great wealth. (*Matthew* 19:21–22)

**Bible Character Joy Lesson #5**

---

God has definite plans for you—plans that include joy. "For we are God's workmanship, created in Christ Jesus to do good works, which God prepared in advance for us to do" (Ephesians 2:10).

Our response to God's commitment to us? "Brothers, I do not consider myself yet to have taken hold of it. But one thing I do: Forgetting what is behind and straining toward what is ahead, I press on toward the goal to win the prize for which God has called me heavenward in Christ Jesus"

(Philippians 3:13–14).

What is the prize? The crown of life waiting in heaven for us and everyone we can take with us. How do we win it? We press toward it by the choices we make—to study God's Word daily, to listen to His Spirit, and to put Him and others before ourselves.

When you received Christ, you became a missionary—in business, at school, at the grocery store, and especially at home. Folks need to see Christ in your life. But don't think you have to be perfect to be a testimony for the Lord. Just ask God for the strength to keep on keeping on. That commitment and the joy it brings will make you a powerful witness.

So stick to the basics. An old Sunday school song says that J-O-Y stands for Jesus first, Yourself last, and Others in between. "May the God of hope fill you with all joy and peace as you trust in him, so that you may overflow with hope by the power of the Holy Spirit" (Romans 15:13).

# 4

# Fuel for Fire

*I* sat halfway up the stadium seats on a beautiful Florida day watching my son pitch a college baseball game.

Behind me, I heard voices—those of a man and a woman—getting louder and uglier. As the conflict escalated, objects starting flying. Soda cans, folding chairs, coolers, and jackets bounced past me down the stadium bleachers.

The lady seemed to be winning. She was the angriest person I've ever seen, and I've seen some angry people. There weren't any signs that alcohol was involved. Just unbridled fury.

After a while, they ran out of things to throw. But they continued to yell at each other at the top of their lungs. Finally, a security guard came to usher them out of the stands.

That only moved the action to the parking lot. They put on such a show that a couple hundred fans lined up at the top of the stadium to watch the fight instead of the game.

During all this, my son had been trying to do his job of

striking out the opposing team. He had no idea what was going on outside the stadium but seemed a little distracted by all of the commotion. Hardly anyone was watching the game.

*It's a beautiful day,* I thought. *We live in a country of freedom and prosperity. We're blessed in so many ways. Those two probably came to the game to cheer for someone they know (hopefully not their son). Why in the world would they be eaten up with such excessive anger?*

Our society as a whole suffers from an absence of joy and an abundance of anger. If you don't believe me, take a drive in a large city like Atlanta during rush hour.

It's amazing how consuming an angry, bitter spirit can be. Even Christians sometimes get caught up in that frame of mind. We become master guardians of our rights, and we're furious when one of them is violated.

Our human nature is somehow attracted to conflict. We are drawn to a good fight. We get a thrill out of watching someone win. And, yes, we can get a sort of morbid pleasure from watching the other guy get whipped. We often get our energy from the adrenaline of getting even.

You wonder who won the fight at the stadium, don't you? I'm not sure. The police eventually came and broke it up, but not before it turned into a fistfight. It was a good thing for the man that the police showed up. That woman had a mean right hook!

We all know the fire of anger that can pour through us like hot lava. But there is a drastically different kind of fire—a fire from God. A joy-fire. It enables any child of God to not just exist but to soar. "But those who hope in the Lord will renew their strength. They will soar on wings like eagles; they will run and not grow weary, they will walk and not be faint" (Isaiah 40:31).

We don't always soar, do we? We'd like to, but we don't. Life hits us head-on, and the collision puts us in a tailspin that can last for days, even weeks.

Have you ever gotten to a point in your life where you were not just running in place but gasping in place? About to die from the harsh realities of life? Emotionally disintegrating?

Such feelings are often a consequence of our instant-everything society. Affluence is almost a given. If we don't have it, something must be wrong. We expect everything to be easy. When it's not, we pull out the mental chain saw and try to rip through the roadblocks keeping us from quick success and happiness.

*Nowhere in the Bible are we told that being spiritual means cowering in a corner, afraid to enjoy living!*

We start taking everything and everybody too seriously. We don't know how to laugh at life's detours. We get chest pains and miserable dispositions. We get furious. Like spoiled children, we kick, scream, and holler at every obstacle in our path.

## BASEBALL AND THE DEVIL

Speaking of spoiled children—and even more common, spoiled parents—some of my most exasperating times in life came when I was a Little League baseball coach. Few things are as frustrating as having the parent of a Little Leaguer act more childishly than the child. And, believe me, they can do it.

I recall a tournament game we were playing. From the stands behind me, I heard, "Not even the devil would make a coaching decision that stupid!" The irate parent repeated his announcement several times.

*Am I that bad a coach?* I asked myself. I knew I should

ignore the outbursts, but I couldn't seem to do it until I told myself, *Oh, Dale, get a grip and stop taking yourself so seriously!*

One of the miraculous things joy does is help us to do just that—stop taking ourselves too seriously. Joy enables us to not sweat the small things while it gives strength to handle the big stuff.

Maybe the devil would never make a coaching decision that bad, but I doubt he'll ever have the joys I've had, either. The devil has a lot to be angry about. We believers don't. We're blessed beyond measure now and headed for a home in heaven.

Whether we're coaching our kid in baseball, having a challenging day at work, or dealing with family problems, we need to learn *not* to be rattled by the everyday irritations of life. We've simply got to stop majoring on minors. Life's too short to waste our joy trying to live in the ideal. And it's too fleeting not to spend some time laughing—especially at ourselves.

We Christians have forgotten how to laugh and have a good time. Nowhere in the Bible are we told that being spiritual means cowering in a corner afraid to enjoy living!

Rather than our joy being contagious, we often cause allergic reactions in people around us. They not only don't want what we have but run as fast as they can away from us, saying, "If that's what it's like to be a Christian, count me out."

Life's not easy. No one is exempt from its detours. There are endless reasons to give in to anger and frustration. But every hard spot and impossibility is accompanied by unique opportunities for joy. "When anxiety was great within me, your consolation brought joy to my soul" (Psalm 94:19). "Be glad for all God is planning for you. Be patient in trouble, and prayerful always" (Romans 12:12 TLB).

You mean, hardship brings joy? Yes! Even the toughest things in life. Hilarious joy. Bountiful joy. Unlimited joy. It is possible to get to the confidence level where you say, "Lord, I know You are going to use this problem to build my faith, which will increase my perseverance. Then I'll be a more mature person—more balanced, more optimistic, more joyful."

If you could learn to have joy in the hard things, what would the rest of your life be like? Hallelujah-city, don't you think? "Dear friends, do not be surprised at the painful trial you are suffering, as though something strange were happening to you. *But rejoice* that you participate in the sufferings of Christ, so *that you may be overjoyed* when his glory is revealed" (1 Peter 4:12–13, italics added).

Get it? Stop acting like a baby when things don't go your way. Instead, start rejoicing. Why? Because you start a joy-cycle.

The more you rejoice by faith, the more you become like Christ. The more you become like Christ, the greater your capacity to be a genuinely joy-filled person. And so on.

The next time you have to change a tire on the freeway, how will you react? Cars race by so fast your teeth rattle. You're sweaty and dirty. The jack won't work. You'll probably be talking to yourself, but what will you be saying?

*Lord, this is great. I'm going to reckon this a joyful experience. I'm even going to thank You for allowing this today.* If you learn to do that, you'll taste heaven. You'll have a power in your life you never dreamed possible.

## SELF-TALK

Not long ago, I was at the dentist's office having a cavity filled—a great big one about the size of the whole tooth. I didn't want a crown because they cost several hundred dollars. So I said, "Doc, just attach a filling to whatever you can find in there."

I seldom ask for anesthesia. To me, the numbness is worse than the pain.

"Fine," he said. "I'm only going to drill for about twenty-five seconds." Just twenty-five seconds.

It was no twenty-five seconds. It was twenty-five years!

I'd been studying about how the joy of the Lord brings supernatural strength, so I figured this was a good time to put it to the test.

The whole twenty-five years he was drilling, I was telling myself, *The joy of the Lord is my strength. The joy of the Lord is my strength.* I must have said it four hundred times.

The good doctor packed that big crevice with filling-goo. After it set for a while, he said, "Bite gently."

Well, I bit a little too hard. I bit that mammoth filling right off!

He sighed. "I'm sorry, but I'll have to re-drill that."

*The joy of the Lord is my strength,* another four hundred times.

Joy is a source of strength even in times of pain or heartache or disappointment. Whatever is thrown at us. Even in the dentist's chair, I was learning more about the art of faith-talk. I was believing the Scriptures that assured me that joy from God is a fuel for fire.

What would happen in our lives if we consistently practiced faith-talk?

"The Lord daily loads me with benefits."

"God the Father, God the Son, and God the Holy Spirit are this very day looking for opportunities to fill my heart with joy."

"Things are happening in my life that I don't understand, but I'm counting all of them as opportunities for joy."

"The joy of the Lord is [my] strength" (Nehemiah 8:10). To have strength, I need joy. But where does joy come from? "You will fill me with joy in your presence" (Psalm 16:11). God will fill me up with joy when I'm in His presence, so how do I get there? "Enter his gates with thanksgiving and his courts with praise" (Psalm 100:4). Praise and thanksgiving bring me into God's presence, so "[I will] continually offer to God a sacrifice of praise—the fruit of lips that confess his name" (Hebrews 13:15).

> I will exalt you, my God the King;
>     I will praise your name for ever and ever.
> Every day I will praise you
>     and extol your name for ever and ever.
>
> Great is the LORD and most worthy of praise;
>     his greatness no one can fathom.
> One generation will commend your works to another;
>     they will tell of your mighty acts.
> They will speak of the glorious splendor of your
>     majesty,
> and I will meditate on your wonderful works.
>                                           —*Psalm 145:1–5*

If we talked to ourselves like that, life would become a celebration of joy like we've never imagined.

Is joy there for me? Yes! Do I have to hunt for it with a magnifying glass? No! "Though you have not seen him, you love him; and even though you do not see him now, you believe in him and are filled with an inexpressible and glorious joy, for you are receiving the goal of your faith, the salvation of your souls" (1 Peter 1:8–9).

God is daily loading us with blessings. It's a fact! Do I see those blessings every day? Do I taste those divine delicacies? Do I instruct my heart in what I should be saying to myself?

"This is a great day, and I really love life."

"The Lord is just bombarding me with blessings right and left."

"It's like my life is a giant funnel, and all these blessings are filtered down on, of all people, me!"

"Well," you may ask, "you're saying I'm supposed to look at life as if it's one big party? Tons of joy and ounces of sorrow?"

Not exactly. Life's got plenty of sorrow. That sorrow is swallowed up, though, in the reservoir of God's goodness. God doesn't trickle blessings to us; He loads them on us.

"Then how come I can't see them?" you ask.

Many of the things that should bring us joy are things we cannot see. They may be invisible because of our poor spiritual eyesight. We could be too distracted to sense them. But they are there. We are surrounded by reasons for joyous living! God is making us spiritually rich—gloriously rich—and we may not even recognize it.

Ever have your Bible open to claim its promises but also have your fingers crossed? That's no good. That's not living in faith.

Revamp your self-talk. "Oh, Lord, I want to walk by faith and not by sight. I want to taste how good You are. How supreme You are. I want to sense these invisible blessings around me. I don't want to be so caught up in the web of my own disappointments that I can't see Your goodness. I don't want to grow ugly weeds of bitterness that choke my disposition. I don't want to be a despondent person. I just naturally walk by sight, so please help me, Lord, to learn to walk by faith."

I'm not saying you become joyful just by deciding to. Instant-joy formulas won't cut it. Magic joy. Silver platter living. No trouble mixed in with the blessings. It doesn't work that way. Joy is stimulated by faith, *not by sight.*

In this you greatly rejoice, though now for a little while you may have had to suffer grief in all kinds of trials. These have come so that your faith—of greater worth than gold, which perishes even though refined by fire—

may be proved genuine and may result in praise, glory and honor when Jesus Christ is revealed. (1 Peter 1:6–7)

Do you consider it pure joy when you fall into all kinds of testing? You can. You can start living above everyday hassles rather than underneath them. Talk about fuel for fire! "Consider it wholly joyful, my brethren, whenever you are enveloped in or encounter trials of any sort, or fall into various temptations" (James 1:2 AMPLIFIED).

---

### Saul Forfeited Joy by Refusing to Obey.

"What have you done?" asked Samuel.
Saul replied, "When I saw that the men were scattering, and that you did not come at the set time, and that the Philistines were assembling at Micmash, I thought, 'Now the Philistines will come down against me at Gilgal, and I have not sought the LORD's favor.' So I felt compelled to offer the burnt offering."
"You have acted foolishly," Samuel said. "You have not kept the command the LORD your God gave you; if you had, he would have established your kingdom over Israel for all time. But now your kingdom will not endure; the LORD has sought out a man after his own heart and appointed him leader of his people, because you have not kept the LORD's command." (1 Samuel 13:11–14)

**Bible Character Joy Lesson #6**

---

How can we possibly consider it totally joyful when we encounter a trial we don't understand or a temptation that looks like it's going to run over us? By faith. And the truth is, sometimes God has to be a little tough on us. Otherwise, we never learn to walk by faith. As long as we walk by sight, joy will be scarce.

"Are you kidding?" you say. "Me? Walking by faith? Me? Not worrying? That seems like a great idea, but how in the world do I learn to do that? My faith is anemic—has been for years."

Faith increases when I begin to comprehend at least a fraction of how great God's love for me must be.

> I pray that out of his glorious riches he may strengthen you with power through his Spirit in your inner being, so that Christ may dwell in your hearts through faith. And I pray that you, being rooted and established in love, may have power, together with all the saints, to grasp how wide and long and high and deep is the love of Christ. (Ephesians 3:16–18)

> Being strengthened with all power according to his glorious might so that you may have great endurance and patience, and joyfully giving thanks to the Father, who has qualified you to share in the inheritance of the saints in the kingdom of light. (Colossians 1:11–12)

## WINNING GIANT BATTLES

For nearly three years, I had the very challenging ministry of encouraging a man held in the grip of homosexuality. Trent had a tremendous desire to be delivered from that lifestyle. He would call me at two or three in the morning, weeping, asking for Bible verses, seeking counsel and encouragement. One day, he'd be determined to beat temptation, and the very next, he'd be certain he was a hopeless case.

"Dale," he said during one late-night phone conversation, "I want the joy on my face that I see on yours. At times when I'm suicidal, at times when I don't think I can ever be delivered from this viper, at times when I've got no hope, I think about your smile and it makes me keep trying."

*Does your smile encourage someone to keep trying? Does it keep a person in the ball game?*

Does your countenance reveal Almighty God, who lives inside you? Does your smile encourage someone to keep trying? Does it keep a person in the ball game? Does the joy inside you fuel a fire of love and compassion that others— no matter how wretched their state—simply cannot deny?

Why not adopt the glorious habit of smiling? It's incredible the impact that even a smile can have on someone's entire life. Why not self-talk so much about the goodness of your God that you can't keep Him to yourself? Why not think about God's goodness so much that you begin to glow, to radiate God's love to folks around you?

You'll still have days when it seems joy is a million miles away. We all do. You'll encounter problems—giants—that you think will hound you to death. But the strength to face those giants is available to us every new day.

I will exalt you, O LORD,
    for you lifted me out of the depths
and did not let my enemies gloat over me.
    O LORD my God, I called to you for help
and you healed me.
    O LORD, you brought me up from the grave;
you spared me from going down into the pit.
    Sing to the LORD, you saints of his;

praise his holy name.
For his anger lasts only a moment,
but his favor lasts a lifetime;
weeping may remain for a night,
but rejoicing comes in the morning.
—Psalm 30:1–5

At some time during our walk down the road of life, we'll all experience the loss of a loved one, a heart-wrenching disappointment, a seemingly unavoidable accident. I wish I could promise you otherwise, but no one is exempt from troubles.

Grief, sorrow, and pain may endure for a time, but God hasn't forgotten you! He knows exactly how heavy that burden is that's sitting on you. He is acutely aware of your heavy heart. He's your heavenly Father. Your defense attorney. Your friend. And He gives you these personal guarantees: "No temptation has seized you except what is common to man. And God is faithful; he will not let you be tempted beyond what you can bear. But when you are tempted, he will also provide a way out so that you can stand up under it" (1 Corinthians 10:13).

What about Christ's intercession to the Father on our behalf?

"I am coming to you now, but I say these things while I am still in the world, so that they may have the *full measure of my joy* within them. I have given them your word and the world has hated them, for they are not of the world any more than I am of the world. My prayer is not that you take them out of the world but that you protect them from the evil one. They are not of the world, even as I am not of it. Sanctify them by the truth; your word is truth." (John 17:13–17, italics added)

His divine crane is able to lift that heavy weight off our weary backs, but there are times, for reasons we may not understand, He chooses not to. That's when we learn that with His Spirit in us no giant, no obstacle, no problem can overwhelm us. Start facing the Goliaths in life with that confidence, and you'll be amazed at your increased joy.

## A MADE-IN-HEAVEN COUNTENANCE

As I prepared for a long flight from Atlanta to Seattle after one of those everything-goes-wrong weeks, I felt down physically and emotionally. When I got there, I was supposed to be the man with the answers and the encouragement, not for just one meeting but for a three-day seminar!

I took a seat on the plane with a heavy sigh. A flight attendant greeted me with a warm smile. She might not have won any beauty contests, but the joy of her countenance struck me. Her face was so radiant, I wondered if she'd glow in the dark.

Later, she'd finished serving meals, and most of the passengers had put their seats back for some shut-eye. As she walked by, I caught sight of her name tag. "Gail," I blurted out, "could I ask you a personal question?"

"Sure." She smiled.

"You know for sure that if you died you'd go to heaven, don't you?"

"Yes, I do," she replied without hesitation.

"I knew it," I said. "Your inner beauty leaves no doubt. If you keep smiling and glowing the way you have on this plane, you're going to have an awesome ministry in many lives."

She looked a little startled but managed a humble, "Thank you." Then she added, "I've only been a believer for a few months."

I told her how I was on my way to Seattle to teach a

seminar and had boarded the plane tired and discouraged. "Your countenance has lifted me right out of the seat of this plane. Because of your ministry in my life, I'm now ready to go encourage some other folks."

She sat down next to me, and for several more minutes we enjoyed uplifting fellowship in the Lord. She became, if it were possible, even more radiant. That was twenty years ago, but I'm sure I wasn't the last person Gail's joy infected.

Whatever joy blockers may have been stalking her that day were having a tough time afflicting her. Her joy—her fire—was so real it warmed me as she talked. She was obviously casting her cares upon her heavenly Father, banking on the promise that He had a ton of love and blessings just for her (see Psalm 55:22; Matthew 6:25; Romans 8:26–27; Hebrews 7:25).

You, too, can count on the fact that each new day there will be sufficient strength—plenty of fuel for your fire—to live in victory. No matter how persistent those "I give up" thoughts might be, don't give in to their persuasions.

*As if God were grace-broke! Fresh out of the supernatural stuff. What makes grace possible in your life is the fact that you don't deserve it.*

If anybody had reason to give up, the apostle Paul did as he endured imprisonment in a cold, dark dungeon at Philippi. Yet, in spite of his circumstances, he sensed plenty of reasons to be uplifted. High on his list were the believers at Philippi. Friends in the Lord were so important to the old warrior of the faith. God gave him the strength not to give up, often through the words or actions of his brothers and sisters in the faith.

Dear brother Christians, I love you and long to see you, for you are my joy and my reward for my work. . . . Always be full of joy in the Lord; I say it again, rejoice! Let everyone see that you are unselfish and considerate in all you do. Remember that the Lord is coming soon. Don't worry about anything; instead, pray about everything; tell God your needs and don't forget to thank him for his answers. If you do this you will experience God's peace, which is far more wonderful than the human mind can understand. His peace will keep your thoughts and your hearts quiet and at rest as you trust in Christ Jesus.

And now, brothers, as I close this letter let me say this one more thing: Fix your thoughts on what is true and good and right. Think about things that are pure and lovely, and dwell on the fine, good things in others. Think about all you can praise God for and be glad about. Keep putting into practice all you learned from me and saw me doing, and the God of peace will be with you.

How grateful I am and how I praise the Lord that you are helping me again. I know you have always been anxious to send what you could, but for a while you didn't have the chance. Not that I was ever in need, for I have learned how to get along happily whether I have much or little. I know how to live on almost nothing or with everything. I have learned the secret of contentment in every situation, whether it be a full stomach or hunger, plenty or want; for I can do everything God asks me to with the help of Christ who gives me the strength and power. (Philippians 4:1–13 TLB)

Abounding in joy may not be easy. At times, it seems impossible. Unless you factor in God's grace. God's grace is greater than all of our sins, sicknesses, and sorrows. God's grace has the divine ability to rise to every challenge. Remember, grace is not earned. That means you may have a hundred reasons why you don't deserve to be joyful. You may think your track record of being lukewarm as a Christian disqualifies you from future joy. As if God were grace-broke! Fresh out of the supernatural stuff. What makes grace possible in your life is the fact that you don't deserve it. It's undeserved mercy.

Grace does for your weary heart what no earthly medicine can. It replaces sorrow with joy. God's grace says, "I know the circumstances of your natural life are impossible. Devastating. Overwhelmingly discouraging. That's why I'm here—to do something supernatural in your mind and heart. I'm here to encourage you—to fill you with courage. So, can you give me one logical reason why you shouldn't be uplifted?"

---

## Caleb Found Joy by Dependence upon God's Guidance.

But because my servant Caleb has a different spirit and follows me wholeheartedly, I will bring him into the land he went to, and his descendants will inherit it. *(Numbers 14:24)*

**Bible Character Joy Lesson #7**

---

I had an amazing experience when I was a kid, sitting on the jetty in front of my home. The water surrounding that sea wall was quite deep, so some really big fish would swim within a few feet of where I sat. My friends and I were watching mammoth ships glide along the Gulf Stream when a large tarpon darted by. Not far behind it was a huge hammerhead shark—well over ten feet long.

Tarpons are great jumpers, and this seventy-five-pounder decided to leave the water and, hopefully, the shark. It soared high in the air, bright silver scales glistening in the tropical sun. I'll bet it was as surprised as we were when it didn't land back in the ocean, but an arm's length from us on the flat part of the jetty.

One of my buddies dashed to the house for a camera. Another guy and I wrestled the fish, still flopping furiously, into our arms for a couple of snapshots. We held onto the big fellow for dear life, grinning from ear to ear.

By that time, the hammerhead had lost interest and decided to look for his dinner elsewhere. We gently lowered our tarpon back into the ocean. It circled for a moment to gain strength, then swam happily away.

The pictures turned out great—two little fishermen holding a very big tarpon caught with their bare hands! Actually, the tarpon caught us. It jumped right into our laps. We didn't fish for it, work for it, or even deserve to have our picture taken with it. That was fishermen's grace.

Get this—God's grace is swimming all around us, just waiting for the chance to jump into our lap and bless us with joy. We don't have to fish for it. All we have to do is be there! Just believe that our God can and will "do immeasurably more than all we ask or imagine, according to his power that is at work within us" (Ephesians 3:20).

## A NEW DIMENSION

Ken was right on the verge of trusting Christ as his personal Savior. "I'm afraid of the unknown," he said to me. "I'm scared of what I might be if I choose to become a Christian."

I was thinking, *Not as afraid as I am for you if you don't choose to become a Christian!* Instead, I drew two circles on a napkin. "Ken, one of these circles represents your life now. The other is a dimension of life you can only have as a member of

God's family."

He listened.

"With that new dimension," I continued, "comes something you don't have right now—true happiness."

"You're absolutely right about that," he quickly responded. "I don't have it now."

"Ken, I'll make you a guarantee. The joy you are eligible to experience, represented by this circle, is a thousand times better than the happiness you are trying to scrape up in the life you now have, in the other circle. Don't be afraid of a life that is infinitely better than the one you already have."

He looked at me for the longest time. Then he nearly shouted, "I'm gonna do it! I'm not going to miss out!"

Friend, stop holding back for fear of what you might become if you get sold out for God. Stop clutching so tightly to earth-life, and start depending on His matchless grace.

Joy is there for you today. And it will fuel a fire within you that'll make every minute of life worth living. It will transform your attitudes, your actions—put you into a higher gear spiritually and take you to an altitude where you can triumphantly soar.

# 5

# Highway Robbery

*T*he guy had been to the Caribbean on a diving trip," my friend, a Miami police lieutenant, told me. "He had a prestigious job. We found a picture of his attractive family in his wallet. From what I gather, he'd been depressed and had hoped the trip would help. But I guess he didn't find any magic happiness in the Caribbean."

"That's for sure," I said.

"Yeah, he went to baggage claim at the Miami airport, took his high-powered spear gun out and tried to kill himself with it. We got a call, and when we got there he was stuck in a stall in the men's room with a spear sticking out of both sides of his neck, but alive."

"You mean, he missed his spinal cord and vital arteries?" I asked.

"The whole ordeal was weird. The spear ripped through his larynx but didn't hit anything life-threatening. We had to turn him sideways to get him out of the bathroom. We couldn't put him on a stretcher, so he had to walk out of the airport with that spear sticking out of his neck."

"Not only did he fail to escape his troubles," I offered, "but he probably had a thousand people gaping at him."

"Yeah," my friend said, "my heart really went out to him. I absolutely didn't know what to say."

That bizarre, sad story shows what can happen to us when we try to earn or buy happiness. That new boat or toy or vacation might buy some momentary cheer. Perhaps. For a fleeting moment. Who knows, we might even make it past the airport with a little momentum, but once we hit the freeway or the office, all the joy we had gained evaporates.

## STRESS RELIEF

On a recent ministry trip to the Florida Keys, I was rewriting this very chapter while "suffering for Jesus" in the cabana next to an oceanfront villa. I noticed a beautiful boat docked at the pier. The words *Stress Relief* were painted on the stern.

Later, as I walked along the dock, the owner of the *Stress Relief* was about to launch off, so I gave him a hand.

"Does it do what its name says?" I asked.

With a sheepish grin, he answered, "About half the time."

About half the time! A gorgeous, expensive toy out on the vast ocean in the beautiful Florida Keys, and it only provides happiness half the time. What do we have to look forward to on the job or at school on the usual dull day? Why is joy so hard to find? And when we do actually latch onto it, why does it slip so quickly from our grasp?

It's because we get tackled by joy blockers. Ruthless bandits. Highway robbers that snatch away this priceless gift. They deceive us into believing they can give us just what our heart longs for, only to leave us empty, even more miserable than we were before.

In my opinion, we Americans who are so rich in things are so poor in joy because of these joy-thieves. I want to list a few of these ugly thieves to watch out for. But before I do, I want to remind you that "the one who is in you is greater than the one who is in the world" (1 John 4:4). Life's joy-blockers are not unbeatable. The God who lives in you is infinitely, immeasurably greater than the most tenacious joy-thief you will ever encounter. The Scriptures explain these joy-blockers and instruct us how to avoid the nasty thieves.

When I was in the building business, I once contracted to build a big, beautiful home for Dave and Debra, a nuclear engineer and an electrical design engineer respectively.

Dave and Debra were two of the most arrogant people I'd ever met. They were sure they knew infinitely more about the construction industry than I did even though they'd never built a home.

It was so impossible to work with them that halfway through the project, I found myself scrambling to settle the ongoing dispute out of court. My company took a large financial setback, but I knew it would get worse the longer I waited. They found another builder who had even less success in satisfying them.

During the months I worked with them, I shared the Lord with them. As you might expect, they saw themselves as not needing God or His forgiveness. They thought they didn't need anyone but themselves, yet if anything in their lives didn't conform totally to their desires, they were instantly consumed by misery.

Since houses, careers, and life in general aren't perfect, Dave and Debra were usually frustrated and miserable—like everyone out there trying to latch onto temporal happiness. The cold truth is that circumstances, marriage, friends, careers, and health are all somewhat roller coaster rides. The good times can be really uplifting. The bad times are just that—bad. People like Dave and Debra who are without Christ don't have anything to hold onto.

Their own relentless drive for success and perfection becomes their god—one that will not allow contentment.

We Christians need to learn an important lesson from the Daves and Debras. We can't go to the god of *me and mine* for fulfillment. Goodies and ambitions are part of life. But even a boat named *Stress Relief* will run out of fuel and leave you stranded in discouragement.

Is that the end of our story? Temporary fulfillment? The fuel of life run dry too soon? Take a stab at happiness and hope for the best?

No way! Joy is not a blessing that comes by chance. We can learn how to prepare our hearts to soak in the joy God gives us.

## JOY BLOCKERS

Just as a disease such as cancer slowly saps the life from a healthy person, certain attitudes—diseases that spring up in our dispositions—effectively block our joy. No one can live very long with malignant cells in his body. They must be cut out. In the same way, the joy-killing diseases must be cut out of our dispositions.

Let's find out what these diseases are, how to successfully remove them, and then how to stay disease free after the ugly stuff is dealt with.

### Hardening of the Heart

This disease can be diagnosed by lack of interest. No hunger for the Scriptures. Little thirst for Christian fellowship. It's a lukewarm Christian—gradually getting cold—caught in the blahs. Don't look to him for joy.

Proverbs 10:28 says, "The prospect of the righteous is

joy." What does that mean? It means that to focus on God, His Word, and others rather than self produces joy. Keep that focus, and your prospects for joy are beyond your wildest dreams.

Hardening of the heart is easy to cure. Do the opposite, and you get the opposite.

> Oh, the joys of those who do not follow evil men's advice, who do not hang around with sinners, scoffing at the things of God: But they delight in doing everything God wants them to, and day and night are always meditating on his laws and thinking about ways to follow him more closely. (Psalm 1:1–2 TLB)

Don't let your spiritual arteries clog up with the cholesterol of indifference. Be willing, in His strength, to resist any thought or attitude that will dampen your zeal for the Lord. Use the weapons of spiritual warfare outlined in Ephesians 6:10–20, and go to war!

## Woe-Is-Me-ism

The guy with this disease has had it rough. He might even be broke. I don't know about you, but I've been there a couple of times. The last thing I felt in that penniless state was joy.

Listen to what Paul said, however, about the people in Macedonia. "Out of the most severe trial, their overflowing joy and their extreme poverty welled up in rich generosity" (2 Corinthians 8:2).

Those Macedonian Christians, though flat broke, were full of joy. They were the opposite of Woe-Is-Me-ism. What was the result of that joy? Instead of sitting around licking their poverty wounds, they were busy ministering to others. That's proof that joy doesn't come from pampering yourself.

It comes when you get outside yourself and start blessing others.

You know what's the worst symptom of Woe-Is-Me-ism? It neutralizes joy. Even if you start your day upbeat, this disease stops it cold. It says, *Look at my life. It's one big heartache after another. Nothing goes my way. Poor, poor me.* It blocks the joy from getting into your heart. Try as you might, you will not manufacture much happiness if you harbor an I'm-a-victim mentality.

## Precious-Me-osis

This disease is frighteningly common and extremely consuming. It plagues the heart, causing the sufferer to become oblivious to anyone else. It's a conscious or unconscious choice to place my wants, plans, feelings, and comforts too high on life's totem pole. It's living by emotion instead of by obedience to God's Word.

Did Paul rebuke Precious-Me-osis? Did he ever! "But none of these things move me, neither count I my life dear unto myself, so that I might finish my course with joy, and the ministry, which I have received of the Lord Jesus, to testify the gospel of the grace of God" (Acts 20:24 KJV).

Paul was not looking to material things in this life to make him happy. Neither was he esteeming life so precious that he lost sight of God's program. He was not even counting on a certain comfort level of earth life. In fact, Paul claimed it was possible to be "sorrowful, yet always rejoicing; poor, yet making many rich; having nothing, and yet possessing everything" (2 Corinthians 6:10).

## Samson Forfeited Joy by Allowing His Emotions to Rule Him.

Then she said to him, "How can you say, 'I love you,' when you won't confide in me? This is the third time you have made a fool of me and haven't told me the secret of your great strength." With such nagging she prodded him day after day until he was tired to death. . . .

Then the Philistines seized him, gouged out his eyes and took him down to Gaza. Binding him with bronze shackles, they set him to grinding in the prison. (Judges 16:15–16, 21)

**Bible Character Joy Lesson #8**

Minister-to-Me-itis

This malady is subtle, and its sufferers are some of the nicest people around. Minister-to-Me-itis victims look good, smell good, and sound good. "You know, I'm so glad that I'm saved and heavenbound."

So, what's wrong with that? Sounds pretty good. Then they continue, "I just love to be around God's children. They encourage me. They hug me. They ask me how it's going at work, at home, at school. I just love being ministered to."

Well, that doesn't sound too bad, does it? I told you this one's hard to pick up.

Over a period of time, Minister-to-Me-itis makes a person spiritually overweight. It's OK for a baby to have a bottle stuck in his mouth, but if he doesn't eventually get out of the crib and start walking, he'll get so fat he can't move.

With this disease, happiness is missing in action because the one afflicted is looking to other people to bring it to him. His potential for consistent joy is limited. Why? Because if you want to gain something in God's economy, you have to give it away.

That's crazy, isn't it? God's ways often seem upside down to our messed-up rationale.

The cure for Minister-to-Me-itis is found in Hebrews 3:13: "But encourage one another daily, as long as it is called Today, so that none of you may be hardened by sin's deceitfulness."

In other words, an attitude adjustment is needed. It's time to start putting others first. Later in Hebrews we find this exhortation: "Let us not give up meeting together, as some are in the habit of doing, but let us encourage one another—and all the more as you see the Day approaching" (Hebrews 10:25).

## Sabbath-Hyper-ism

We are busy people, aren't we? Busy, busy, busy. What about Sabbath rest?

As Sabbath-Hyper-ism creeps in, we find ourselves too busy to take a break. What we fail to consider is that erratic Sabbath rest will eventually put a major squeeze on our joy. Things like building a deck, playing tennis, taking in a pro ball game, or making a trip to the mall are OK things to do, but they hardly strengthen our inner being. Even God rested, and He instructs us to do the same.

No strength—no joy. No joy—no strength! It's the joy-cycle in reverse.

Take time to Sabbath. Even if you sometimes have to do so in halves or thirds. If your schedule is crazy, as mine often is, take two half days or three one-third days to spend time with God, with yourself, and without a demanding agenda.

You'll be amazed at the blessings that come your way because you set aside time for God.

Take a long walk. Go on a picnic. Spend time on the back porch or in a solitary corner at the library. Find out what works for you. Make a commitment to Sabbath each week, and God will give you wisdom to creatively carry it out.

There remains, then, a Sabbath-rest for the people of God; for anyone who enters God's rest also rests from his own work, just as God did from his. Let us, therefore, make every effort to enter that rest, so that no one will fall by following their example of disobedience. (Hebrews 4:9–11)

These are only a few of the joy-blocking diseases. Lots of things compete for the right to deliver the knockout punch, to put out our joy-lights. The oppressors may appear to be people, problems, or circumstances. In truth, though, the culprit is our own attitudes—the ways our minds get off-center and away from God's game plan.

Don't despair. Keep reminding yourself that "greater is he that is in you, than he that is in the world" (1 John 4:4 KJV).

## CLIMBING OUT OF THE PIT

Rich and I had known each other since high school. After years of occasional phone calls, we agreed to meet at a weekend men's conference where we hoped to hear penetrating and uplifting messages from gifted Bible teachers.

We both needed it. Each of us had just been through some degrading treatment by fellow Christians. Though a thousand miles separated us, we were amazed at how parallel our stories were.

We had a lot of wounds to lick. But we found ourselves doing more whining than healing. We complained about the lack of organization at the conference, we fussed about the air-conditioning in our motel room, we criticized our waitress. By the second day, I was feeling so troubled and exhausted, I left the meetings early.

I was on a negative roll, and so was Rich. We were fueling each other's fire, but it wasn't a fire of joy, it was a wildfire of negative thinking.

*Dale, I told myself, you're allowing the unfairness of life to flatten you. Life went the opposite direction from what you thought it should, and now you're just plain refusing to get over it. You know that negative thoughts are draining. No wonder you're discouraged. Remember, "As [a person] thinks within himself, so he is" (see Proverbs 23:7 NASB).*

Rich was an analytical person by nature, so his wounded spirit burned even hotter than mine. The way he had been treated by other Christians was really bugging him. Honestly, I could hardly blame him for the way he felt. Still, I realized it was doing him no good.

"Rich, I've been doing some thinking."

"Dale—thinking?" he interrupted. "That's scary."

"Terrifying," I agreed.

The laughter that followed was much-needed medicine for both of us.

"Rich," I continued, "I tend to plan life. I can see how things ought to be orchestrated. In fact, I've got a lively imagination, and I can really put the future together nicely—in my head."

Rich laughed again.

"When things don't go as I've planned, and the orchestra's playing out of tune, I can get pretty grouchy, right?"

His grin faded as I said, "Your struggle is people who act or react out of selfishness, running over their friends and loved ones in the process. That's what gets under your skin."

"So, we're grumpy old men."

"Not yet, I hope, but we'll become grumpy old men if we don't get a handle on our attitudes. I think we need to agree together to get on with life. To look first at the good in the way the orchestra is playing—and in the way people are behaving."

"Yeah, you're right," he said. "Life's way too short to come up short on joy because we're busy being irritated at the shortcomings of people and circumstances around us."

Both of us agreed to make a change. And, right then, we sensed a new lease on life.

"I'm ashamed to admit it," I concluded, "but I think the bottom line is, we expect life to be smoother and easier than it is."

*He had the maximum benefits life could offer, but his joy-o-meter barely registered zero.*

Let me say something to you thinkers, you prophets who see life the way it ought to be, and you discerners who try to figure out the why of things. There's a time and a place for reasoning. Don't stop being who you are, but don't forget to live, either.

If you'll use some of your wisdom to search out the good in life, in people and in circumstances, the steamroller of gloom won't run over you. Besides, the smile you'll wear from discovering the joys around you will provoke a few other folks to wonder what's on that perceptive mind of yours.

Rich and I had slipped into a negative mentality and developed a downer mind-set. All of us get discouraged at times about things—often about things that haven't even happened yet. In Ecclesiastes, Solomon illustrated just how low this negative thinking can take a person. He had the

maximum benefits life could offer, but his joy-o-meter barely registered zero.

His exasperation was well-expressed: "Light is sweet,
and it pleases the eyes to see the sun. However many years a
man may live, let him enjoy them all. But let him remember
the days of darkness, for they will be many. Everything to
come is meaningless" (Ecclesiastes 11:7–8). Solomon was
saying that you'd better enjoy everything you can find in
life because pleasures are short and shallow.

I don't like dark times. Do you? In fact, I dread them. But
they will come, so we need to keep them in perspective.
Earth-life is temporary. It's a journey, not a destination.

God has equipped us to influence others with the fire of
our joy-filled spirit. We are called to build His kingdom. We
are called to drive out darkness with the power of His glorious light.

For much of his life, Solomon missed the boat. Let's not
join him! His philosophy: "I'm going to live to please myself." Hey, I'm far from the wisest guy who ever lived, but
even I know that's not going to make you happy. You're *not*
going to find a toy, goal, or cause on this earth—no matter
how hard you work at it—that will bring you the level of
joy God offers.

The frustrated king said: "So then, banish anxiety from
your heart and cast off the troubles of your body, for youth
and vigor are meaningless" (Ecclesiastes 11:10). It's almost as
if he was saying, "Don't get bogged down in the negative—
in trying to gratify self—like I did. Go the other way!"

This and other Scriptures prove that it is possible for the
heart—the seat of our emotions—to produce enormous
amounts of joy. How's your heart doing?

Ask yourself this question: *When I look at life, what do I see?*
If it's mostly imperfections, you're in big trouble. This life is
crammed with imperfections—things that bother us about
ourselves, others, society, church, kids, work. The list is

endless. If we stay entrenched in what life *ought* to be, we are destined to be stressed-out, bitter persons. Remember, you are either going to get *bitter*, or you're going to get *better!*

I listened as a lady shared with me some convincing reasons for her frustrations in life. After hearing her case, I said, "You know what I think? I think you're rating your life every hour by the hour."

"What do you mean?" she questioned.

"Every hour or so you are comparing your last hour of life with what a perfect hour should have been. You're living in a constant state of frustration and emotional energy drain because you are obsessed with how you'd function if you and life were both perfect."

She thought about that for several moments and then exclaimed, "No wonder I'm exasperated. I'm beating myself to death because I'm not perfect. As the day goes on I realize I'm even further from where I'd be if I were perfect. That creates misery heaped upon misery!"

She then made a potentially life-changing determination. "I'm going to stop comparing reality with the ideal. I'm going to start loving the day—no matter how far from perfect my circumstances might be."

*It's time to stop wimping out—wishing and hoping for some miraculous overnight circumstance to deliver happiness.*

## MAGNETIC MAX

Just after our church was founded, we had a family visit us that was going through hard times. Max had recently been swindled out of his business by a not-so-honest partner. The other guy disappeared with all the money, and Max was left saddled with all the debt. He was battling desperately to find a foothold financially as well as emotionally.

The folks in our church tried to give as much moral support and financial help as we possibly could.

One thing I'll never forget about Max was his laughter. What a hearty and contagious laugh he had! My struggling attempts at humor from the pulpit were greeted with his booming laughter, which made others want to laugh along with him. For a while, I actually envisioned myself a gifted joke-teller. Before and after a church service, you'd hear Max's laughter.

Many Sundays, after a long week of harassment from creditors, he'd come to church with barely enough money for gas to make it home. But none of that dampened his ability to taste the lighter side of life. Max had plenty of reasons to be an angry, depressed person, but he didn't buy them. Instead, he chose joy.

Every church needs a Max. If you happen to be one, let 'er rip! Your exuberance will not only convince people that joy is possible, it will light a fire in some of them that will deeply affect their lives.

It's time to stop wimping out—wishing and hoping for some miraculous overnight circumstance to deliver happiness. It's time to start catching those joy thieves red-handed. Lock 'em up and have 'em handcuffed to some gloomy prison wall where they can't steal another ounce of your precious joy.

## OVERLOADS

Here's the bottom line: Does everything have to go your way for you to be really happy?

If so, you're in for a long wait. Probably a lifetime. Joy is meant to be more than an earthly commodity. It transcends the frailty of life. And it's yours for the taking. No power or person can snatch it from you—not unless you let it go or

give in to one of the spiritual diseases or bandits that so
swiftly siphon it from you.

God designed you to experience joy. So don't put a dark
cloak around your heart. Take the king's advice. "Let your
heart cheer you in the days of your full-grown youth" (Ecclesiastes 11:9 AMPLIFIED).

Speaking of youth, what is your typical attitude toward
things you can't change? The older we get, the more things
there are in life we can't change.

A high school student sees an endless life stretch out
ahead of him. "Just wait and see what I do with my life," he
says. "I'm not only going to be successful, I'm going to retire
at forty-five. Just watch me."

By the time he reaches forty-five, he's saying, "I'm just
happy to be alive and get a paycheck every week."

Next thing he knows, the years begin to zip by and he
realizes the course of life is irreversibly set. Aging, infirmity,
loss.

Somewhere along life's road, he has a critical choice to
make. Will he fight to swim upstream against the direction
life's river flows, becoming angry and exhausted by the effort? Or will he learn to go with the flow—resisting evil but
not resisting the course of life? Accepting those things that
he can't change will be the key.

One thing he must learn along the way is that he's not
the general manager of the universe. And neither are you or
I. Pity the poor perfectionist who thinks he is.

I always smile when parents with young children look at
other people's kids and say, "My children are *never* going to
act like that." I try to remember to pray for those idealists
who are in for a surprise. The joys of good parenting are
many, but miserable will be the perfectionistic parent who
anticipates a sinless child. He'll be sadly disappointed. Kids
just don't come wrapped that way. Control freaks either die
young or end up frustrated with a disheartened family.

If you're a control freak, get over it. The happiness you might glean from pushing or tugging until something goes your way is slim pickin's compared to the joy of resting in God's sovereign rule. "We wait in hope for the Lord; he is our help and our shield. In him our hearts rejoice, for we trust in his holy name. May your unfailing love rest upon us, O LORD, even as we put our hope in you" (Psalm 33:20–22).

In his penetrating book *Margin*, Dr. Richard Swenson identifies twenty-three areas of life that tend to run over us. He calls this Overload Syndrome. I won't list those overloads, but you could probably identify several of them.

Overloads—often good and noble responsibilities— swamp us. Smother us. Emotionally bury us. It's no wonder we're starving for joy. We're too busy, too overburdened to enjoy true happiness. It's a struggle to even find the time to read a book telling us how to experience consistent joy!

Be diligent, yes. Work hard, yes. But leave the results, the promotions, and the income levels to almighty God. He is very capable of handling all of that without you.

When you let Him handle the things in life that are beyond your control, your joy level will skyrocket. He will bring a person or circumstance into your life to encourage you at the very moment you're ready to give in to despair. He is a loving, faithful Father. Always.

## ELECTRIFYING POWER

Allow me to shift gears for a moment. We often shrink from talking about things that unnerve us. Things like the powers of darkness—and I don't mean nighttime; I mean spiritual wickedness.

We must face these issues, though. The Bible clearly speaks of principalities, powers, and rulers of darkness and their mission to rob us of our victory in Christ.

Why should they do that? Because their purpose is to

steal, kill, and destroy. Pretty frightening, huh? It would be, except that they were trodden upon by Christ on Calvary's cross. So why should we cower at the very thought of evil forces when they're already defeated?

Diane, a girl who visited our church, didn't know that Christ had already put the forces of evil under His feet. She needed direct intervention from God. She was demon possessed—I mean taken over.

Just nineteen years old, she was a shy person by nature. But when the demons would exhibit their control of her hundred-pound body, she was strong enough to lift a heavy oak table right off the floor with one hand, while lying flat on her back!

Our whole church got involved in praying and ministering to her. When we first commanded the demons to identify themselves, these eerie words came from her mouth: "We are Legion, for we are many." My hair went from a brushed-back style to an electrified Afro in two seconds!

There's a lot I could tell you about the next seventy-two hours. But I'll just say the bad guys lost and almighty God prevailed!

Once Diane was purged of the evil spirits and born into God's kingdom, she was amazingly changed. There was a large scar on the left side of her face that she had always hidden by keeping her hair in front of her face. For the first time in years, she pulled that hair back and smiled at everyone.

Diane went from terrifying to electrifying overnight.

My faith got some reconstructive surgery through that experience. I learned three major things from her deliverance. (1) If there is that much hatred in the world of darkness (and, believe me, hatred was so prevalent in her that at times it was difficult for her to breathe), how much *loftier* must be the love of our wonderful God? (2) If the satanic world is drenched in gloom and misery to that depth, then what are *the heights* to which the joy of the Lord could take us? (3) If there is such staggering power in the hands of the rulers of darkness, how much more *dynamic* is the power that resides inside God's children through the Holy Spirit?

*Patience says, "I will not assume*
*responsibility for God's problems, nor*
*will I decide on His timing."*

Do you believe that you and I need God's power to live victoriously in this life? Do we not need that enablement, especially when we are being assaulted by joy robbers—the circumstances or even the demonic forces around us?

We've already discussed some of the tangible things God's resurrection power does for us and through us. So let's use it. Let's live in victory because of it. Let's count on it.

### HIGH GEAR

Remember, endurance and patience usher in joy. When you find a joyless person, you will inevitably find a quitter—someone who retreats too easily. Joy and patience—not quitting—go hand in hand.

We are instructed to count it all joy when everything in our life goes opposite from the way we would like. "Prepare your minds for action; be self-controlled; set your hope fully on the grace to be given you" (1 Peter 1:13).

Patience says, "I will not assume responsibility for God's problems, nor will I decide on His timing." When I say *God's problems,* I don't mean there are situations God can't handle. I mean I've given control of my problems to Him—not one of which is the least bit of a surprise to Him.

We might define worry as *impatience with God and His program.* When I worry, I'm simply being impatient with the

how, when, where, and why of God's plans for me. I'm saying, "God, You haven't fixed this yet, and I'm not one bit
happy about it. I have every right to this big scowl on my
face. And since You can't handle things, I'll just handle this
myself, thank you."

That kind of attitude will smother joy every time. "But," you
say, "I'm a genetically inherent worrier. I was born worrying. For
generations, my family have been accomplished worriers."

I'd bet you're genetically impatient, too. And I'd guess
that elevated levels of joy aren't in your genes. Listen, you
can only blame so much on your physiology. Today is a
good day to hurdle those genes and start living like the supernaturally empowered person you are in Christ.

Our society of the twenty-first century cultivates impatience. Look at the way people drive in traffic. Watch them
at work. Spend a few hours observing young people at
school. Catch a few advertisements on TV.

One commercial shows people eating a two-for-the-
price-of-one pizza, laughing and having fun. The next tells
you how to have a slim, attractive body. And both say you
deserve it *now*. What they don't say, though, is that demanding everything now will never bring you lasting happiness.
As long as impatience is on the rise, joy is on the decline.

My life starts undergoing a blessed transformation when
I say, "Lord, I'm Yours. My problems are Yours. I'm going to
just wait for You to do *whatever* it is You want to do in me,
around me, and through me."

That's when God's power kicks into high gear in us.

For God, who said, "Let light shine out of darkness,"
made his light shine in our hearts to give us the light of
the knowledge of the glory of God in the face of Christ.
But we have this treasure in jars of clay to show that this
all-surpassing power is from God and not from us. (2
Corinthians 4:6–7)

## Job Found Joy by Refusing to Give in to Negative Circumstances

After Job had prayed for his friends, the LORD made him prosperous again and gave him twice as much as he had before. All his brothers and sisters and everyone who had known him before came and ate with him in his house. They comforted him and consoled him over all the trouble the LORD had brought upon him, and each one gave him a piece of silver and a gold ring.

The LORD blessed the latter part of Job's life more than the first. *(Job 42:10–12)*

**Bible Character Joy Lesson #9**

The Scriptures tell about a prosperous man named Job who lost everything—wealth, family, reputation. I can't comprehend the degree of loss Job sustained, but I know that losing everything does hurt. Deeply. I've been there.

Sandwiched between my two pastorates were twelve years of business and seminar teaching. I spent five rewarding years with Christian Financial Concepts teaching workshops on money management. I was the expert who instructed people in dozens of communities across America about managing their resources. Losing everything seemed impossible to me. I had the knowledge to keep such a thing from happening in my life. Or so I thought.

God led me to leave the financial ministry and plant a new church and, at the same time, start the construction business I've spoken about. I built dozens of homes over the next five successful and fulfilling years. Then it all came to a screeching halt. Interest rates skyrocketed, and the homebuyers' market dried up. I was caught holding the bag—four unsold, unrentable houses. My financial walls came tumbling down.

Joy was nowhere in sight. I'd lost everything I'd spent a lifetime working for—my business, my retirement, even my home. My confidence as a man took a major hit. To a large degree, my spiritual fire went cold.

That dark time continued for months on end. I became impatient with God, with myself, with my circumstances, with the people in my life. My joy ship had hit a reef, and it was sinking. The more impatient I became, the faster I descended toward rock bottom.

A negative mental-emotional-spiritual outlook is complicated by the absence of strength, because no joy means no strength. Think about a time when you were going through a period of joylessness. Let's not even call it depression. You couldn't muster an ounce of happiness. You focused on the gloomy side of life. And you got up the next day and the next after that with a discouraged spirit, believing things would never be any better.

Perhaps you were like me, stubbornly fighting for your self-esteem but always losing. No energy. No strength. No enthusiasm. There is no denying it—when joy is missing, life is a major bummer. But don't stop reading. I finally realized I was pumping bullets into my own foot—or brain, actually.

I had to make a huge choice. Was I going to get bitter or better? I could continue to allow bullheadedness to drive me into the rut of pessimism, or I could remind myself, "In all things God works for the good of those who love him, who have been called according to his purpose" (Romans 8:28).

I wonder how often we quote Romans 8:28 and then act as if we don't really believe it. A key to gaining confidence in its truth lies in knowing what comes earlier. "I consider that our present sufferings are not worth comparing with the glory that will be revealed in us" (Romans 8:18).

So, right away, I began shouting, "Oh, hallelujah! Let's go celebrate the wonderful goodness God has sent my way. What a happy, humbling experience! Job said, 'Naked I came from my mother's womb, and naked I will depart' [Job 1:21]. Looks like I'm way ahead of him. I'm back to having nothing long before I die. Flat broke. Praise the Lord!" Right? *Not exactly.* I was too busy licking my wounds to praise.

Eventually, though, I did come to thank Him for allowing me to lose everything. At first, I had to thank Him strictly by faith. Now, in retrospect, I can thank Him by sight as well.

Because of that experience, I have a different attitude about things—possessions, the American dream. My grown children readily admit they are less materialistic than they were before the experience. I enjoy their commitment to the Lord, especially their willingness to give generously to God's kingdom.

What, then, shall we say in response to this? If God is for us, who can be against us? He who did not spare his own Son, but gave him up for us all—how will he not also, along with him, graciously give us all things? . . . Who shall separate us from the love of Christ? Shall trouble or hardship or persecution or famine or nakedness or danger or sword? (Romans 8:31–32, 35)

That's a theology you can stake your life on. You can look at the nasties and the uglies and the joy thieves eyeball to eyeball and say, "You are *not* going to get me! I *know* that my God is, this very moment, at work. He's *using you*, you nasties, uglies, and joy thieves, to make me more like His Son."

That's the kind of stuff I had to come to grips with to

start moving forward in my journey to joy. *I had to get emptied of me that I might be filled with Him.* I had to get emptied, not just of the security of things, but of things. Period. The absence of things opened the door for contentment to come in. "Keep your lives free from the love of money and be *content* with what you have, because God has said, 'Never will I leave you; never will I forsake you'" (Hebrews 13:5, italics added).

That's how to deal with the thieves clamoring to snatch away joy. Tell them, "Hey, don't get some wild idea you're getting to me. These troubles aren't even a minor irritation when compared to the big picture of God's kingdom. I'm not buying your negative garbage."

### ARREST 'EM AND JAIL 'EM

Tough times *force* tough choices. Whichever way we choose, there's a domino effect. My lousy attitude had fostered a chain reaction of misery. When I finally admitted that, daylight appeared at the far end of the tunnel. I started asking God for a blessed—instead of bitter—domino effect.

In the middle of that everything's-caving-in experience, new thoughts bombarded me. God was asking me questions, and I was answering.

He caused me to see that I had to make some huge attitude adjustments, beginning with a humble and grateful spirit. Next He started giving me megadoses of assurance of His faithfulness.

I was reminded daily that my choices carry a lifetime impact. "See to it that no one misses the grace of God and that no bitter root grows up to cause trouble and defile many" (Hebrews 12:15).

Opening our eyes to God's goodness stops the joy-thieves right in their tracks. The power and authority to arrest and jail those highway robbers are yours as God's child.

"Now if we are children [of God], then we are heirs—heirs of God and co-heirs with Christ, if indeed we share in his sufferings in order that we may also share in his glory" (Romans 8:17).

Earth-life is tough, no doubt about it. It comes packaged with sorrows and disappointments. So keep your focus on heaven. Things may be absolutely stinky right now, but God is at work. He's turning your stinkies into sweet-smelling blessings. *He loves you. Yes, you!*

Just be patient. Don't lose heart. Don't allow the highway robbers to overtake you. To sit on top of you. To pound you into the dirt. Stary claiming this promise: "Great peace have they who love your law, and *nothing* can make them stumble" (Psalm 119:165, italics added).

# 6

# A Steamroller
# or a Chariot

*I* played high school football with a big ol' boy named Chris.
I knew he had a tough home life and needed a friend. So,
occasionally, I'd spend the night at his house.

His parents were alcoholics and violent when intoxicat-
ed. On a typical night, his father would come in at two or
three in the morning and start a fight with his mother,
which normally led to fists flying. I remember hearing objects and even bodies thrown across the room.

When Chris and I were awakened by one of these scuf-
fles, we'd lie awake in silence until the fireworks subsided,
and then for hours afterward.

Chris handled all of this in a quiet sort of way, but I
knew it was carving deep and lasting wounds in his heart.
He drifted through high school in quiet hopelessness.

There's nothing more miserable than being miserable.
Chris's parents made choices. They chose to be miserable.
Whatever excuse we may offer, the bottom line is that we
choose to react the way we do.

Before you get irritated at me, let me explain what I mean. Circumstances can be beyond our control, but our attitude never is. We have a choice in our lives to follow the joy route or the misery route.

Every day, people around us—Christians included—choose to succumb to the attitudes of this sick world we're temporarily parked in.

Let's you and I decide not to give in to life's pressures. Not to be consumed by selfish ambitions. Not to be steamrolled by a world in the hands of the wicked one (see 1 John 5:19–21).

The lousy condition of the world around us does pose a huge challenge, but there is a guaranteed source of victory—our faith. "For everyone born of God overcomes the world. This is the victory that has overcome the world, even our faith" (1 John 5:4). "The Lord your God is in the midst of you, a mighty One, a Savior—Who saves! He will rejoice over you with joy" (Zephaniah 3:17 AMPLIFIED).

## ROAD RAGE

One sultry afternoon, Atlanta's beltway, I-285, was backed up for miles. A frustrated driver in the long line of traffic gave a sour look to the man in the car beside him. Without hesitation, the man drew a gun and fired through his open window at the unsuspecting victim, who died in the hospital a few weeks later.

Road rage is a growing phenomenon. It's not the only emotional imbalance around us, though. We live in a frustrated society. An angry society. An illogical society. A despondent society.

The perplexing question is, *How can I be a positive person in a negative world?*

I know the answer—reprogram my thinking to line up with God's instruction manual. "Do not conform any longer to the pattern of this world, but be transformed by the renewing of your mind" (Romans 12:2).

God promised it in the Old Testament. He proved it in the New Testament. His Word never fails. "So shall My word be that goes forth out of My mouth; it shall not return to Me void—without producing any effect, useless—but it shall accomplish that which I please and purpose, and it shall prosper in the thing for which I sent it" (Isaiah 55:11 AMPLIFIED).

My thought patterns start getting reprogrammed when I start digging in His book.

Open my eyes that I may see
    wonderful things in your law. . . .
My soul is weary with sorrow;
    strengthen me according to your word. . . .
Turn my eyes away from worthless things;
    preserve my life according to your word. . . .
Let your compassion come to me that I may live,
    for your law is my delight. . . .
May my lips overflow with praise,
    for you teach me your decrees.
            —Psalm 119:18, 28, 37, 77, 171

The prophet Jeremiah had a curious way of telling us about the relationship of joy to God's Word. "When your words came, I ate them; they were my joy and my heart's delight, for I bear your name, O LORD God Almighty" (Jeremiah 15:16). I doubt he literally *ate* the Scriptures, but I'm certain he read them and digested their truths in his heart!

The here and now won't always be sugarcoated. But there are answers to life's challenges. There are scriptural answers, and, yes, there are practical answers too. But those answers don't come easy. In difficult moments, or months, we must discipline ourselves to walk by faith. To resist the spirit of despair. To look to Him for strength to deal with the circumstances at hand.

Some days drag by with no magical Scripture verse. No still small voice. No friend in sight to bring encouragement. Those days are so hard. At times, they seem to pile endlessly on top of each other, despair heaped upon discouragement.

Just remember, though, that dark days won't last forever. God is still on His throne. He hasn't run low on grace or goodness. "And the God of *all grace*, who called you to his eternal glory in Christ, after you have suffered a little while, will himself restore you and make you strong, firm and steadfast" (1 Peter 5:10, italics added).

A steamroller to flatten you emotionally, or a chariot to lift you above the stronghold of life's oppressors? Every single day you choose one or the other.

## DREAM BARBER

Did you ever wake up from a troubling dream that seemed so real you wondered if it had actually happened? It was in color. You remember words and even facial expressions. I recently had one so real I wrote it down.

I enter a hair salon and take a seat in one of the chairs. This ornery little barber with a fiendish grin begins working on my hair. I watch in the mirror as he cuts huge hunks out of my hair and then starts to shave me completely bald!

"What are you doing?" I scream in horror.

I take a good look at the barber—it's Johnny Harrison, one of the leaders in our church teen group!

"I'm the barber," he says in this arrogant tone. "You do what I say." He has this look on his face that says, "I'm totally in charge here."

So he's working on what little hair I have left. All of a

sudden he goes, "Yuck! Yuck! Yuck!"

In a half-sleeping, half-waking state, I wanted to wake up and end this crazy dream. But I also wanted to hang in there and see what was going to happen. Maybe I could embarrass Barber Johnny in front of the whole church to get back at him.

Then he yells, "Look at this! You've got little mice in your hair!" Johnny holds up this tiny mouse-guy by the tail. "Nesting in there!" he gasps in disgust.

"Oh, no!" I say. "What do I do now?"

His smirk gets bigger. He's really loving being in charge. "Here's the treatment plan. You've got to do this for a whole week."

"What do I have to do?"

"Get some gray sand and mix it into mud." He smirks. "Mat your hair with it real good. Put on a shower cap and wear all that for a week. Then come back and see me. I'll shampoo your hair and those little fellows will be all gone."

That's when I woke up.

I dare you to interpret that one.

Some days our lives make about as much sense as a crazy dream. About the only thing we can figure out is that we can't figure out anything. Bizarre circumstances. No hope of change. Stooped shoulders. Heavy heart. Everything so hazy, so unclear. The steamroller's about to flatten us again.

That's not the end of the story, though. "Surely it was for my benefit that I suffered such anguish. In your love you kept me from the pit of destruction; you have put all my sins behind your back" (Isaiah 38:17).

Sometimes God allows the steamroller to come chugging our way just to get our attention. Sometimes we need to get leveled flat on our back—run over by life—to snap us back to spiritual reality. To show us how much we have to be thankful for and how few reasons we have to fuss over ourselves.

## ONE POWERFUL SMILE

I often read about or meet people who have every reason to be languishing in depression but they're not. People with physical, emotional, psychological, or circumstantial problems more overwhelming than anything I'm going through with my small problems and limitations.

These are special people. People who choose to fuel their lives with joy in spite of obstacles I can hardly imagine. There are multiple millions of people on this planet who have every reason to proclaim, "My life is utterly steamrolled. I have no reason to live. Not *one* reason to be happy." Yet millions of those precious people refuse to stay spiritually or emotionally flattened. Instead, they choose joy.

I was spellbound as I read a story about a lady with rheumatoid arthritis. Her face was frozen into a twisted scowl, and so was her heart. Her self-talk convinced her daily that she would always be a miserable cripple.

At the brink of utter despair, the thought came to her, *What if I tried to smile—even for no reason—just to smile?*

Her face was so taut and twisted that even moving her facial muscles was extremely painful. But she refused to give up on the idea that smiling might somehow change her life. It took many tedious days of working at it before she could get her muscles to engineer a smile. Once the smile did come, she embarked on a daily program of smiling at everybody she saw.

Whether she realized it or not, she was putting into practice a profound proverb: "Commit thy works unto the LORD, and thy thoughts shall be established" (Proverbs 16:3 KJV).

Guess what? Her smile began to soften that hardened heart inside her. A once-despondent attitude took giant strides for the better. Soon, miraculous changes occurred in her health. Her body began to respond to the joy that was bathing her spirit.

Her doctor categorized those physical improvements as spontaneous remission. He told her they were probably only temporary and warned her not to be surprised if her previous condition returned. *Thirty years later,* no one around her doubts the power of a smile! There are some things we *can* change.

A few days after reading that amazing story, I had my own pity party in full swing. It was an authentic poor-me banquet. Since I didn't want to be anywhere near people, I ate my McDonald's cheeseburger while sulking in my car. A van parked next to me, and I sensed someone staring at me.

*Go ahead and stare,* I thought. *Maybe you're having a crummy week, too.*

Finally, I couldn't resist the impulse to look. My eyes met those of a severely disabled little girl. And on her face was the biggest smile I had seen in months.

Time seemed suspended. Her sunny expression, in spite of her circumstances, rebuked me no end. *OK,* I thought, *you win.* And I smiled back at her.

That caused her smile to spread so wide it could have jumped right off her face. And she just kept on smiling and smiling.

I kept smiling, too, as I drove away and mouthed a thank-you to her.

Joy can make a day wonderful for a little girl who may not understand much but somehow knows the power of a smile. Joy can take somebody crippled and ready to give up and make her a whole new person. If joy can do that for people in intense physical or emotional pain, it ought to have a heavy-duty influence in my life. It ought to light a fire in me that shouts, *"I'm unstuck here, no longer swamped by the pressures of life. And I'm seated there—next to Jesus—and I'm loving every minute of it."*

People who endure great hardship really do snap our heads around, don't they? They slap us in the face with the reality of just how *few* reasons we have *not* to be joyful. Beyond the natural tendency to compare our circumstances with theirs, though, they help us see life with a resurrection perspective.

They remind us there's more to come after this life.

Therefore, we do not lose heart. Though outwardly we are wasting away, yet inwardly we are being renewed day by day. For our light and momentary troubles are achieving for us an eternal glory that far outweighs them all. So we fix our eyes not on what is seen, but on what is unseen. For what is seen is temporary, but what is unseen is eternal. (2 Corinthians 4:16–18)

God's power brings victory over death. The joy of knowing that God personally can be counted on to give us daily strength was forever guaranteed when He conquered death. "It is for freedom that Christ has set us free. Stand firm, then, and do not let yourselves be burdened again by a yoke of slavery" (Galatians 5:1). "Cast all your anxiety on him because he cares for you" (1 Peter 5:7).

You may have endured depression for a period of time, but don't lose heart. God's book of promises has encouragement custom-written just for you. "Your statutes are my heritage forever; they are the *joy of my heart*. My heart is set on keeping your decrees to the very end" (Psalm 119:111–12, italics added).

## Joseph Found Joy by Entrusting His Circumstances to God.

When Joseph's brothers saw that their father was dead, they said, "What if Joseph holds a grudge against us and pays us back for all the wrongs we did to him?" . . .
His brothers then came and threw themselves down before him. "We are your slaves," they said.
But Joseph said to them, "Don't be afraid. Am I in the place of God? You intended to harm me, but God intended it for good to accomplish what is now being done, the saving of many lives. So then, don't be afraid. I will provide for you and your children." And he reassured them and spoke kindly to them.
(*Genesis 50:15, 18–21*)

**Bible Character Joy Lesson #10**

Part of the chemical makeup of joy, though, is that it has to be supernaturally recharged. A dose of Scripture today won't carry me through tomorrow. Each day as I read the Word, meditate on it, and apply it, the injection of joy straight to my downcast spirit revitalizes my disposition.

How do I know God will revive my joy? Simply because *God said it!* "Your statutes are my heritage forever; they are the joy of my heart" (Psalm 119:111).

Are you missing joy in your life? Do you sense that far too often you are being flattened by the ups and downs of life? How much time are you spending in His Book? How much time are you investing in that guaranteed source of joy?

I meet people all the time who tell me, "Life's such a bummer, a real drudgery."

"Well," I usually reply, "when was the last time you spent forty-five minutes really poring over Scripture—just loving it and letting it minister to you?"

"Um, it's been several weeks, I guess," is usually the timid answer. No wonder they're starving. No wonder there's no joy in their lives.

> *High-road traveling demands that we look at people, places, and things from the positive.*

One of my high school teachers, Coach Jenkins, surely needed something to counteract his negative spirit. Coach J. was the master of put-down. Whether on the basketball court or in the classroom, his philosophy was that if you put somebody down enough, he will react positively and apply himself more.

Funny thing—actually *sad* thing—I don't think his method ever worked. Not even once.

The irony of it was that he thought he was a pretty cool guy. He laughed at his own sarcasm. He imagined himself a big man on campus. But when he entered a room or walked up to courtside, the temperature—figuratively speaking—dropped noticeably.

You rarely saw a smile on his face. Coach Jenkins was an expert at spreading gloom, and he didn't even know it!

Remembering Coach J. reminds me that there are really only two roads when it comes to a philosophy of life. He chose the low road—the one where you view people, places, and things from the downside. That's the road of discouragement. Sadly, it's the road most traveled. Any one of us can easily slip into that rut.

We don't have to go that way, though. It takes discipline, but we can travel the high road. High-road traveling demands that we look at people, places, and things from the positive.

The high road is a joyful road. The scenery is fantastic. The rest stops are awesome. The people we meet along the way enrich our lives immeasurably. The effort it takes to stay on the high road is always worth the blessings that accompany it.

Give it a try. Once you get on the high road, you won't ever want to cruise the low road again.

The high road is not without its troubles. In fact, it has obstacles, just like the low road. But high-road trials lead to high-road blessings. An old theology professor of mine used to say, "Count on it—before every blessing comes a test. The tougher the testing, the bigger the blessing!"

## FOILED AGAIN

A few years ago, my daughter Julia was ready to go to a small college in Tennessee. We didn't have the money to send her, but we were confident she was supposed to attend there.

I had an aunt who wasn't all that close to our family. We had little contact, and I wasn't even sure where she stood spiritually. We had less and less in common as the years went by.

Just a couple of days before Julia was to leave for school, a letter arrived in the mail from that aunt along with a check for five thousand dollars. "I want you to have this money," she said. "I'm not sure why, but I feel compelled to send it."

Talk about a celebration in Crawshawville! The whole clan jumped around the living room, filled with joy and thanking God. We could have bounced off the walls because God had supernaturally provided when there were no other options, and just in the nick of time.

The adventure didn't stop there. My finances weren't making a swift comeback, so the following year we were again far short of the money Julia needed to return to school. It seemed likely she wouldn't be able to re-enroll. Again, two days before the final deadline, the impossible happened.

A retired minister friend called me and said, "Dale, I've been praying about your family. I particularly want to know how Julia's doing."

"She's well," I said. "Hoping to return to college."

"What does *hoping* mean?" he questioned.

"Well," I began slowly, "she may have to drop out for a semester or so."

"Why?" he persisted.

"We don't have the money to pay the bill," I reluctantly answered.

"Don't take her out of school yet," he said.

I appreciated that dear friend's interest, but I knew he didn't have a large sum of money. He probably didn't have fifty dollars to spare with the budget he lived on. But I thanked him for his concern and also thanked the Lord for friends who cared so much.

The next day, he called again. "I know a man who has a heart for the college Julia attends," he said. "He loves to help people in situations like hers. A few moments ago, he wrote a check to the school for the entire amount she will owe for the next semester."

We hadn't told anyone of her special need except to ask for prayer from close friends, people who were as broke as we were. We didn't want to humanly manipulate. God is the God of the impossible as much today as He was when He parted the Red Sea. He proved Himself to the Crawshaws—again! More celebrating. More bouncing off the walls. More rejoicing.

*I wonder if God didn't say to Himself, "Bet you didn't think I could work three straight. Just watch this."*

We'd seen the big ugly steamroller coming down the street. It was revved up, ready to make a burnt pancake out of us emotionally. No chance. Foiled again! God's miracle chariot whisked us away at the very last moment. The steamroller of despair was sent reeling in reverse!

Before long, my youngest daughter, Natalie, was ready for college. Now we would have two girls in college on our very limited income. Natalie soon encountered the same predicament Julia had faced. It looked like she'd have to drop out at the midterm break.

You'd think we'd have adjusted to God's never early, never late way of doing things. Hardly. It's so difficult to walk by faith. We certainly had God's track record fresh in memory. But would He—could He—do it again?

I wonder if God didn't say to Himself, "Bet you don't think I can work three straight. Just watch this."

He did it again! A praise-wildfire caught at our house. Our joy knew no bounds. Just plain jubilation. Why? We saw God at work. We celebrated His goodness.

God must smile at our tension when we get ourselves in a pickle. He isn't running low on miracles—not even close. "O Sovereign Lord, you have begun to show to your servant your greatness and your strong hand. For what god is there in heaven or on earth who can do the deeds and mighty works you do?" (Deuteronomy 3:24).

## TAKE YOUR SEAT

"Hold on," you're saying. "It's easy to be excited when things turn out well. You get the unexpected check in the mail. You get the promotion at work. Your doctor says your ailment is something minor. Easy to find reason for joy then. Tangible blessings. But what about when you hope in vain for the check, or someone else gets the promotion, or the doc says *cancer?*"

That's exactly what God's book is for. When your well is dry with no showers of blessing on the horizon, He creates miracle streams in the desert.

> Say to those with fearful hearts,
>     "Be strong, do not fear;
> your God will come,
>     he will come with vengeance;
> with divine retribution
>     he will come to save you."
>
> Then will the eyes of the blind be opened
>     and the ears of the deaf unstopped.
> Then will the lame leap like a deer,
>     and the mute tongue shout for joy.
> Water will gush forth in the wilderness
>     and streams in the desert.
>
> —Isaiah 35:4–6

That's when faith will carry you—faith that He meant what He said. By faith, tell your heart, "Whoa, there's joy in this Book, and I can experience it *consistently*. I'm sick and tired of being emotionally squashed by my circumstances. This Book says I can sit *on top of them rather than them sitting on top of me.* I'm *not* going to get steamrolled. I'm going to rise above these disappointments."

Remember, whatever life throws out, we can taste joy. We are eligible to shout, "Hallelujah! I know I have the victory because I'm clothed in the righteousness of Jesus Christ." "Therefore, if anyone is in Christ, he is a new creation; the old has gone, the new has come! All this is from God, who reconciled us to himself through Christ and gave us the ministry of reconciliation" (2 Corinthians 5:17–18).

*When life threatens to run over you,
run to God.*

Maybe you can't have your devotional time in the morning because you're barely breathing and you're not sure what planet you're on. You have to crawl to the school bus or office. OK, mornings are out. What about your lunch break? Find a place. You might be surprised at a special place God will help you discover to spend time with Him. Perhaps the best time might be when you get home from work or school. Or right before you go to bed.

However you have to do it, make time to get into God's Word. Your disposition will improve. Your optimism will soar. You'll discover the spiritual stamina to lighten up, loosen up, and really start living.

Life is full of unpredictable turns, things that can snatch your joy from you so fast it'll make you dizzy. But you're a child of the God not even death can defeat. You're already on the winning team. "'Where, O death, is your victory? Where, O death, is your sting?' The sting of death is sin, and the power of sin is the law" (1 Corinthians 15:55–56).

When life threatens to run over you, run to God. Claim His promises and say, "I thank You that You are the God of all grace. I praise You that I will become a better servant through the disappointments of this life. My deepest wounds will be swept away by Your touch."

A few years ago, I visited the transplant ward of a large medical center in Little Rock, Arkansas. Many of the patients shuffled down the hallway looking like they might not survive the ordeal they'd just gone through. Most would never have the kind of lifestyle they had once enjoyed.

I knew that my deteriorating kidneys might land me in a similar predicament within a few years. Reality was clawing at my emotional being. After hours of soul-searching, I made myself some promises.

*I am going to taste each and every day. I'm going to live each day fully. I'm going to say and experience, "This is the day the Lord has made; [I will] rejoice and be glad in it" (Psalm 118:24).*

Since then, when every cell in me clamors to give in to discouragement, I remind myself, "*Why, you do not even know what will happen tomorrow. What is your life? You are a mist that appears for a little while and then vanishes*" (*James 4:14*). And then I tell myself, Dale, "*Be joyful always; pray continually; give thanks in all circumstances, for this is God's will for you in Christ Jesus*" (*1 Thessalonians 5:16–18*).

Often, I tell folks that one of the biggest blessings in my life is my slowly failing kidneys. Why? Because I'm constantly reminded of the temporary nature of life. I constantly work to keep a healthy perspective. I remind myself that *today* is the best day for me to live life to its fullest.

Perspective is so important. When we take health, or family, or freedom to worship for granted, we usually lose focus on our Creator and Sustainer.

The joy portion available to ungrateful people is meager indeed, so let's refuse to be one of them! Let's get mentally and spiritually seated in the heavenlies—our real home and the place where the Lover of our souls awaits our arrival. "Set your minds on things above, not on earthly things. For you died, and your life is now hidden with Christ in God" (Colossians 3:2–3).

## AN OFFICIAL BAND-AID

Over the years, my hearing loss has created some hilarious scenarios. It was especially traumatic for me in high school. Teens love to laugh at one another. I remember the day my world government teacher, Dr. G., said, "Name an official in Bangkok."

He was looking at me when he asked, so I figured I was supposed to do something about it. I immediately got up from my desk and hurried out of the room. I walked rapidly to the school office and asked the school nurse to give me something—something I took back to the classroom. When I walked in, the teacher stopped the class and stared as I handed him a Band-Aid.

Confused? So was he. Instead of, "Name an official in Bangkok," I had heard, "Dale, go to the *office* and get a *Band-Aid.*"

For the next twenty minutes, that quick-witted teacher exercised an astonishing array of verbal fun and games at my expense until he had the entire class in hysteria. Some of my classmates left their desks to roll on the floor in laughter. I was so embarrassed I thought I was going to die.

There are times in life when we have to get tough and turn that emotional steamroller into a chariot. Easier said than done, right? The steamroller had backed over me several times in those excruciating moments. I felt as flat as the coyote in the Roadrunner cartoon. But something inside me said, "Seize the moment. Don't leave this room a loser."

So I stood up and took several dramatic bows. I decided it was all right to laugh at myself, and it was even OK to be the object of other people's laughter. For at least a day, I became the hero by making us miss a whole hour of Dr. G's boring lectures.

People can run over us, can't they? They flatten us with their words, behavior, indifference, ungratefulness, selfishness, and endless other letdowns. And how they love to ridicule.

Hear this: No people pressure or life disappointment has the power to deliver the knockout punch on your joy without your permission. But the question must be asked, "How do I find joy when even the Christians around me give me so many reasons to be discouraged?"

Dig deeper and stop looking to people to meet your joy-needs. Go straight to God's throne and say, "Lord, I know it doesn't make sense for a Christian to act in anger or selfishness toward another believer (and especially toward *me*), but please, help me choose joy, not bitterness. I do now, by faith, give You my people-hurts.

"And, furthermore, Lord, I don't ever want to treat anyone else that way. I know from Proverbs 29:25 that the fear of man is a snare. You alone are the great joy-giver. So I come to You for the encouragement, the strength, and especially the grace I need at this moment. I'm hurting—mortally wounded, it seems. But I *know* Your grace is sufficient, even when it's my brother or sister in Christ who has inflicted the wounds."

You can pray that prayer knowing you have divine strength *planted within you* by God's Holy Spirit. That strength never leaves you because His Spirit never leaves you. Think about who you are in Christ and what He's done for you. He *is* your hope, your peace, your joy, in *every* circumstance—including the people-hurts that tend to obliterate your joy.

> *Take your position as a joint heir with Christ. Get your focus off what others are doing or saying and onto Christ.*

It's time to start banking your emotional stability on His never-failing promises:

> But now in Christ Jesus you who once were far away have been brought near through the blood of Christ. For he himself is our peace, who has made the two one and has destroyed the barrier, the dividing wall of hostility. (Ephesians 2:13–14)

I pray also that the eyes of your heart may be en-
lightened in order that you may know the hope to
which he has called you, the riches of his glorious inheritance in the saints, and his incomparably great power
for us who believe. That power is like the working of his
mighty strength, which he exerted in Christ when he
raised him from the dead and seated him at his right
hand in the heavenly realms, far above all rule and
authority, power and dominion, and every title that can
be given, not only in the present age but also in the one
to come. (Ephesians 1:18–21)

One reason we must learn to rely on promises like these
is that, in our crystal-clear way of looking at things, we can
readily envision the way life *should be* and how people *ought to
act*. But when it comes to ourselves, our vision can be a bit
clouded. Right? "I'm such a loyal employee." Or, "I'm such a
good friend." Or, "I really work at being an encouraging person." Or, "I read my Bible and try so hard to do right."

You may be a wonderful person. I pray you are! But don't
look to your own goodness as your source of fulfillment.
You must, each new day, stand firm in the authority you
have as God's child. And often that means being willing to
stand alone. Do that, and I guarantee the thermometer of
joy will climb dramatically in your life.

Take your position as a joint heir with Christ. Get your
focus off what others are doing or saying and onto Christ.
Start believing that you can grow spiritually to the point of
rising above—literally leaping over—the people-hurts, the
pressures, the circumstances of life.

"As for God, his way is perfect;
    the word of the LORD is flawless.
He is a shield

for all who take refuge in him.
For who is God besides the LORD?
And who is the Rock
    except our God?
It is God who arms me with strength
    and makes my way perfect.
He makes my feet like the feet of a deer,
    he enables me to stand on the heights."
                                            —2 Samuel 22:31–34

## MIND YOUR OWN BUSINESS

"But," you protest, "people aren't going to go away. People-hurts are not going to disappear. I can't ignore them." No, you can't simply pretend they don't exist. You can, however, develop a mind-set that will stop life's steamroller from flattening your joy.

Learn the art of minding your own business! That's a key to disabling the steamroller of despair.

Remember, you're a handful all by yourself! If you learn to transfer the time you spend trying to control others into soaking in God's presence and His blessings, you'll be surprised at the results. Your renewed heavenly focus will eliminate a major portion of the people-instigated insanities you used to experience.

A codependency support group was meeting to share victories and defeats. Melanie told her encouragers of an important step she'd taken in her fight against addiction. "I had such a terrible childhood, and I realized that I've been searching ever since for people who would really care about me."

Her discovery? "I'm very quick to take inventory of how other people are behaving or treating me. I've put a stop to that. I've decided to take inventory of myself to make sure I have my own priorities right and have my focus on the

Lord."

Then she continued with a smile, "What a difference it's making in my attitude. I'm so much happier minding my own business and keeping my eyes on Him."

---

### Uzziah Forfeited Joy by Being Consumed with His Own Agenda.

But after Uzziah became powerful, his pride led to his downfall. He was unfaithful to the LORD his God, and entered the temple of the LORD to burn incense on the altar of incense. . . .
Uzziah, who had a censer in his hand ready to burn incense, became angry. While he was raging at the priests in their presence before the incense altar in the LORD's temple, leprosy broke out on his forehead. (2 *Chronicles* 26:16, 19)

**Bible Character Joy Lesson #11**

---

Stay heavenward focused, and even the giant storms of life will not be strong enough to blow you away! "The LORD is my strength and my shield; my heart trusts in him, and I am helped. My heart leaps for joy and I will give thanks to him in song. . . . The angel of the LORD encamps around those who fear him, and he delivers them" (Psalms 28:7; 34:7).

When I was in elementary school, Hurricane Donna struck the middle islands of the Florida Keys with winds of one hundred eighty-five miles per hour. The damage was unimaginable. Unless you had witnessed it firsthand, you could not possibly envision what the wind, huge seas, and tornadoes did to those beautiful islands.

People lost homes, businesses, fishing boats, life savings, everything.

It seemed impossible, but over the next three or four years, most of what had been destroyed was rebuilt.

Just five years after Donna hit, another giant storm, Hurricane Betsy, inflicted her fury on those same islands. Again, the destruction was absolutely beyond belief.

I'll never forget the day I was helping a businessman burn the remains of his grocery store that Betsy had ravaged. I must have looked disheartened, because he said, "Dale, we built it back before, we'll build it back now, and we'll build it back again if we have to." He smiled a confident smile and added, "Life's too short to waste on discouragement."

I was fifteen then. That optimism made a lasting impression on my life. His I-refuse-to-give-up attitude mirrored that of thousands of others on those islands who rebuilt again and again with undying hope.

Yes, those storms were like giant steamrollers that flattened the Keys. A lot like the storms that come into our lives emotionally—storms that pin us to the ground and run over us with such fury that we can't even imagine a way to rebuild our shattered lives.

Those brave people chose to rise above anguish and despair to rebuild what was leveled to the ground. As a child of God, you can do even better. You can ride the chariot of God's power so high above your problems, they're barely visible! They may have once been devastating, but they now seem small from your lofty vantage point.

Joy elevates you into your heavenly seat. It allows you to ride in God's chariot of fire where "neither death nor life, neither angels nor demons, neither the present nor the future, nor any powers, neither height nor depth, nor anything else in all creation, will be able to separate [you] from the love of God that is in Christ Jesus [your] Lord" (Romans 8:38–39).

A steamroller or a chariot? Which will you choose?

# 7

# Trade It In

*I* have a special talent for acquiring lemons—not the kind you make lemonade with but the kind that stay in the auto repair shop. Having less than the world's biggest budget to work with has somewhat defined my choices. Still, I am a very accomplished lemon-finder.

I remember my 1960 Plymouth Valiant. Actually, it was one of my rare choices that ran pretty well. It had one glaring shortcoming, though. It seemed to invite other cars to crash into it.

I had the kind of insurance that asked for two repair estimates and then sent a check directly to me. A light bulb switched on in my head—Dale in the part-time car body repair business!

We were just barely covering the bills with two toddlers and a third child on the way. I actually started welcoming crashes! One good dent meant a couple months of groceries and a backyard Bondo job by Dale! Give me a hammer and some Bondo and I can make a dent look worse than it started out!

One day, I was backing out of a parking place and glanced to my right. I could see that the driver at the far end of my row wasn't paying a bit of attention to where she was going. I hurriedly shifted into drive to get back into my parking place.

You know how your mind thinks extra fast when adrenaline is flowing? Well, mine was saying, *C'mon, baby, go ahead and smack me. That'll be another two months of groceries!*

And smack me she did!

It was a slow impact—no one hurt. But it was my third insurance check and my third Bondo job in a year. God provides in mysterious ways!

After my horrendous dent-fixing and two terrible paint jobs, that poor Valiant looked like it had rolled off a cliff.

Talk about feeling beat up—the apostle Paul suffered dents and bruises far worse than my old Valiant.

> I have worked much harder, been in prison more frequently, been flogged more severely, and been exposed to death again and again. Five times I received from the Jews the forty lashes minus one. Three times I was beaten with rods, once I was stoned, three times I was shipwrecked, I spent a night and a day in the open sea, I have been constantly on the move. I have been in danger from rivers, in danger from bandits, in danger from my own countrymen, in danger from Gentiles; in danger in the city, in danger in the country, in danger at sea; and in danger from false brothers. I have labored and toiled and have often gone without sleep; I have known hunger and thirst and have often gone without food; I have been cold and naked. (2 Corinthians 11:23–27)

With all of that trouble, I'd say Paul needed extra angels.

I'm sure he had plenty, but God didn't choose comfort as a path to his spiritual maturity! I wish I could say God uses the School of Ease, not the School of Hard Knocks, to spur our spiritual growth. I can't tell you that. But I can assure you God's presence is available even during life's darkest times.

## A NOSY DOCTOR'S PRESCRIPTION

Early in my ministry, I struggled with a mysterious illness. For two long years I'd felt worse than awful. No strength. No energy. Each day I found myself having to fight with every ounce of determination just to keep from giving in to despair.

On top of feeling rotten, we were way behind financially. Having to drag myself to the table with zero appetite wasn't much fun. But dragging myself there day after day to eat zucchini casserole—free zucchini from a friend's garden because that's all there was to eat—was very hard to rejoice over.

My kids were being great sports about it, trying to smile when they wanted to gag.

A lousy circumstance, and no end in sight.

"Uh, Dale, you're about to tell me that joy can even be found when the world caves in and lands on top of me?"

Yep. I'm about to tell you just that. But not with pat answers, simple formulas, or platitudes like "Just do it."

It's not easy. In fact, it is humanly impossible!

But you serve an awesome God. A God of the impossible. A God who intended a victorious spirit to prevail in His children. A God who adopted you into a supernatural system. "The kingdom of heaven is like treasure hidden in a field. When a man found it, he hid it again, and then in his joy went and sold all he had and bought that field" (Matthew 13:44).

Get this. God will creatively design a way to bless your

little discouraged heart at the time you feel least blessable. Here's how He did it for me.

I was sitting in the doctor's office with a screaming child who desperately needed a tonsillectomy. Her crying unnerved me, and I was screaming, too—screaming inwardly because I knew I had no earthly way to pay for the surgery.

Dr. Lefkoff, a little man with a twinkle in his eyes and a big smile, did a second take at me. "You look awful," he said.

"I feel well below that," I replied weakly. Actually, I felt one slippery step from my deathbed. I explained my symptoms.

"This isn't my area of specialty," he said, "but I believe I know what's wrong with you. Want some help?"

Did I ever.

A barrage of tests confirmed a rare blood infection. There was no real treatment available, except the advice he gave me. "Take three weeks of bed rest," he said, "and after that, get a bicycle and start riding a couple of miles a day."

*He's absolutely crazy,* I thought. *Bike two miles? I can barely walk from the bedroom to the bathroom.*

"And you need a more positive attitude, my friend," he continued. "Trade in your negative thoughts for positive ones. Play more and worry less. You are going to get better. Tell your body that often."

I was desperate, and his optimism was contagious. So I took his advice. I made room for a little prayer closet under my basement stairs. I started going to that closet several times a day to talk to God and trade in my "I'll never feel good again" attitude for "I will get better."

Time in that prayer closet became a refuge for me. Some days, I hardly had the strength to pray, so I listened. There were days I simply lay there curled up in a fetal position. I know that at those times, His Spirit interceded for me. Though too down physically to be aware of it then, I grew spiritually during those times.

The first day with the bike was really a joke. I pushed it from the house to the road. There I lay in the grass for half an hour then weakly pushed it back to the house. The next day wasn't much better. By the end of the week, though, I actually managed to lean against a tree rather than lie in the grass.

I couldn't see how lying beside the road or leaning against a tree could possibly help, but I kept doing it. Each day—more prayer, more positive thoughts, a few yards farther down the street on the bicycle. Eighteen l-o-n-g months later, I remember thinking, *Hey, I'm doing better. Thank You, Lord, for Your touch and for prompting that kind doctor to reach out to me.*

## A GRIP ON JOY

Because of the depths of despair I sank to during that illness, I think I've tasted a little of what Paul must have felt.

To keep me from becoming conceited because of these surpassingly great revelations, there was given me a thorn in my flesh, a messenger of Satan, to torment me. Three times I pleaded with the Lord to take it away from me. But he said to me, "My grace is sufficient for you, for my power is made perfect in weakness." Therefore I will boast all the more gladly about my weaknesses, so that Christ's power may rest on me. That is why, for Christ's sake, I delight in weaknesses, in insults, in hardships, in persecutions, in difficulties. For when I am weak, then I am strong. (2 Corinthians 12:7–10).

What we are about to discuss is hard medicine to swallow. It's a vital principle for dynamic living, though. In this important biblical truth is fuel to fire us even in the very toughest times of life.

*It's the principle of exchange. We must learn to exchange—to trade—our weaknesses for Christ's strength.*

Perhaps we're preoccupied with a string of life failures. Or poor health. Or good health. Or possessions. Or always needing to be in control. Or with a certain level of success. The challenges of life tend to consume us. There is no challenge or difficulty, however, that cannot be traded for contentment. These attitudes that imprison our minds need to be put on His altar, left there, and exchanged for something incomparably better—joy.

You may wonder, "How does joy actually provide strength? How can it help me in the blatant disappointments and harsh realities of life?"

Let me ask you something. Have you ever known a truly joyful person who lacked energy or vitality? I can't remember meeting one. Did Jesus lack energy? Zeal? Spiritual stamina? Chew on this: "For to be sure, he was crucified in weakness, yet he lives by God's power. Likewise, we are weak in him, yet by God's power we will live with him to serve you" (2 Corinthians 13:4).

In other words, my weaknesses are not *my liability* but *God's opportunity.* When my reliance on good health or good friends or a good job gets crucified, a vacuum is created inside me that God is anxious to fill with His strength and His joy.

We don't have to wait, though, until our world crumbles to grow in grace. The process happens as we learn to *delight in all things,* even those we would normally despise.

> *"I'll exchange my weakness, my failure, my physical hurt, my psychological struggle, my career disappointment, my heartache for Your strength."*

Just a few days ago, I asked a friend, "Are you happy

about life when it goes your way?"

"Well, sure I am," he said.

"All right. Think about this past week at your job, at home, and with whatever projects you've got going. On a scale from one to ten—one being nothing's going right and ten being everything's perfect—what kind of week have you had?"

"Oh, about a five."

"So that means," I mused, "fifty percent of the time you weren't smiling. You weren't on top of your circumstances. You weren't upbeat. You weren't encouraged or encouraging. You looked a little pouty, a bit depressed."

He just looked at me, visibly stunned.

"What if you had taken the parts of your week that were absolute downers and delighted in them?" I asked. "What would your week have been like then?"

Long pause. "Well, I suppose I'd have an enviable life. I guess I'd be the kind of person that would cause other people to say, 'Whatever he has, I want it!'"

"That's right," I said. "So why not give that kind of living a try?"

The funny thing is, the whole time I was exhorting him to choose joy, the Holy Spirit was pounding me with the same challenge.

For a person to get a daily grip on joy, I believe a literal exchange process needs to occur. I say, "Lord, this is the crummiest part of my week—the worst in several weeks, actually. So I'll do two things. I'll delight in the week I'm having. I don't feel like it, but I'll do it by faith. Second, I'll exchange my weakness, my failure, my physical hurt, my psychological struggle, my career disappointment, my heartache for Your strength."

I trade in the worst part of my week for the best part of Him. My opportunity to make such an exchange with God is far more than just wishful thinking.

When my anxious thoughts multiply within me,
Your consolations delight my soul.

—Psalm 94:19 NASB

I waited patiently for God to help me; then he listened and heard my cry. He lifted me out of the pit of
despair, out from the bog and the mire, and set my feet
on a hard, firm path and steadied me as I walked along.
He has given me a new song to sing, of praises to our
God. Now many will hear of the glorious things he did
for me, and stand in awe before the Lord, and put their
trust in him. (Psalm 40:1–3 TLB)

## WORST TO BEST

When everything is going the way I want, I tend to by-
pass the Lord. It's when I'm weakest that He's strongest in
my life.

"Oh, Father, look at the discouraging news I got from
the doctor."

"Lord, I feel so lonely at school."

"God, it's next to impossible to scrape up money for
even half these bills."

In those times, I can exchange the worst things about
my world for the best things about His. "God, I claim *Your*
strength, *Your* grace, *Your* enabling power. I claim *Your* creative ability to make my worst become my best."

That's why we can rejoice in our weaknesses, or our failures, or even our most impossible predicaments. "Surely it
was for my benefit that I suffered such anguish. In your love
you kept me from the pit of destruction; you have put all my
sins behind your back" (Isaiah 38:17).

*I can spend my life wallowing in the mud of self-pity, or I can wade out into deeper water where God wants me.*

What happens to our weaknesses when we exchange them? That's God's business. I've been anointed with oil and prayed over numerous times for the healing of my kidneys. It may come soon. Or, in God's wisdom, some other scenario may be in the works—a kidney transplant or dialysis or even heaven. The important thing is, *whatever* is impossible or even painful about my health can be *exchanged* for His strength and counted as a *reason* to be joyful.

I can spend my life wallowing in the mud of self-pity, or I can wade out into deeper water where God wants me— where He can minister to me and through me. No matter what comes, God's presence at His altar of grace can fill me with joy.

> Then will I go to the altar of God,
> to God, my joy and my delight.
> I will praise you with the harp,
> O God, my God. . . .
>
> You have made known to me the path of life;
> you will *fill me with joy* in your presence,
> with eternal pleasures at your right hand.
> —Psalms 43:4; 16:11, italics added

What weakness or pain or impossibility do you need to trade in for His strength? What has been robbing you of joy? What things in life have been running over you, flattening you spiritually and even physically?

These things no longer need to have dominion over your spirit. Whatever they are, start exchanging them for God's best. Not just occasionally but on a day-by-day basis.

Say, "Lord, there's not much energy here today. There's not much strength, and there's a lot of pain. There's disappointment, and there's heartache. There are impossibilities. Right now, I exchange all of this for Your divine enablement."

Don't stop there. Keep talking. "Lord, I don't just want to trade in this awful stuff, I want to do it with delight. Lord, I glory in the infirmity You've allowed me to have, because without it I wouldn't have anything to trade in for Your strength!"

---

### Martha Forfeited Joy by Allowing Earthly Tasks to Dull Her Spiritual Senses.

As Jesus and his disciples were on their way, he came to a village where a woman named Martha opened her home to him. She had a sister called Mary, who sat at the Lord's feet listening to what he said. But Martha was distracted by all the preparations that had to be made. She came to him and asked, "Lord don't you care that my sister has left me to do the work by myself? Tell her to help me!"

"Martha, Martha," the Lord answered, "you are worried and upset about many things, but only one thing is needed. Mary has chosen what is better, and it will not be taken away from her." (*Luke 10:38–42*)

**Bible Character Joy Lesson #12**

If we were perfectly healthy, financially secure, and everything was going the way we planned, we'd seldom be asking for God's special grace. We'd be self-absorbed and oblivious to anything but our own agendas, and we wouldn't even get to first base as far as true happiness is concerned. In the case of my kidneys, God may have already chosen to heal them. Or He might say, "Dale, my grace is sufficient for you. Just keep exchanging your weakness for My strength. You'll get everything done that you're supposed to. You'll live as long as you're destined to. You'll experience all the fullness of life I've intended for you."

## THE AMERICAN WAY

It was a dreary Monday. I was sitting dejectedly in the corner of the Corner Café, feeling very sorry for myself. Rain was forecast for the whole week, and the blues were raining on me. My construction crew was home asleep, some of them on payroll rain or shine. In a good week, we could meet our cash flow demands. But a week like this? Trauma-city.

I saw a builder friend across the room. He was eating a hearty breakfast and laughing just as heartily.

*What's the deal?* I thought. *He ought to be just as depressed as I am!* After a few more minutes of my not-very-enjoyable pity party, I could stand it no longer. I strolled over to his table.

"Jim, it's going to rain all week," I said. "How come you aren't in the dumps?"

He laughed. "I know where you're coming from. I used to have a larger company like yours. It was draining me dry. Life seemed to be sitting right on top of me."

He had my undivided attention. "So?"

"So, I canned it. I canned the moving and shaking. I told the Lord that if He'd help me make it as a small fish, I'd give more time to Him, to the Bible, and to my family."

"So?" I said again.

"So I only build one house at a time. I'm out of the rat race. I don't make as much money, but everything is simplified. And weeks like this don't hit me so hard. Plus, I'm keeping my commitment with the Lord, and I wouldn't trade that for anything."

He was right, and I knew it. I determined to act on his wisdom. It took some financial losses—major ones—and significant lifestyle adjustments, but I learned how wise he was.

It's highway robbery—the American way of life. Goodies, goodies, and more goodies. Keep up with the Joneses, who aren't happy in spite of their affluence. Credit. Instant stuff.

Laughter? Peace of mind? I don't see a whole lot of those accompanying the American way, do you?

Don't get me wrong; things aren't bad in themselves. In the same chapter of the Bible that says, "The love of money is a root of all kinds of evil" (1 Timothy 6:10), God has more to say. It's not the money but the mind-set that's the problem.

> Command those who are rich in this present world not to be arrogant nor to put their hope in wealth, which is so uncertain, but to put their hope in God, who richly provides us with everything for our enjoyment. Command them to do good, to be rich in good deeds, and to be generous and willing to share. In this way they will lay up treasure for themselves as a firm foundation for the coming age, so that they may take hold of the life that is truly life. (1 Timothy 6:17–19)

Different strokes for different folks. Just make sure your strokes don't cause you to focus on possessions or careers or investments so much that His kingdom becomes fuzzy. Lose kingdom-focus and you lose joy. Lose joy and you're poverty-stricken. Spiritually, emotionally and physically broke. Bottom line: *Don't let the good life keep you from the awesome life.*

## THE RIGHT TO BE RIGHT

Is there something in your life that smells like an NBA player's feet after four quarters of basketball? When something besides God dominates your life, it's like a bad odor filling a room. Maybe you're just plain consumed with yourself. What really stinks is you! All you can think about is good ol' number one. You're getting in the way of God's blessings. You're robbing *yourself* of joy. You need to exchange *you* for *Him*. Take your ego off the throne and tell Him, "You, God, are the Lord and the motivator of my life, my plans, and my future."

The apostle Paul hit the nail on the head when he concluded:

> But whatever was to my profit I now consider loss for the sake of Christ. What is more, I consider everything a loss compared to the surpassing greatness of knowing Christ Jesus my Lord, for whose sake I have lost all things. I consider them rubbish, that I may gain Christ and be found in him. (Philippians 3:7–9)

You may need to say, "Lord, what is the dominant part of me? The stubborn, willful part that fights to run the show no matter what? That part of me isn't really strength; it's weakness. That's what's getting in the way of my fellowship with You. It's terribly difficult, Lord, but I put it on the altar. I want Your grace, Your joy, Your strength in its place."

Not long ago, I was speaking in south Florida about this *exchange principle*. Afterward, as I talked to people and signed books, I noticed a successful-looking gentleman apparently waiting to talk to me. After the crowd thinned, he walked up and introduced himself.

"I wish I'd heard this years ago," Roberto said, still smiling, "but I had to learn it the hard way. After my second heart attack, I realized that Roberto was getting in the way of everything—including joy. I discovered something revolutionary."

"What was that?" I asked.

"I discovered that unless I yielded the right to be right, I was going to spend a great deal of time being miserable. And so were the people around me."

"Come again?" I said.

"When a person has even a taste of success in life," he explained, "rights easily become master—the right to be successful, the right to have things go as planned, the right to be appreciated, rewarded, even the right to be right."

He looked at me expectantly to see if I was getting it. I nodded, and he continued.

"After facing death for the second time, I finally learned to let some things go—even when I was dead right—and focus instead on being an encourager, to learn what it means to be a giver."

I shook my head again.

"My life changed so radically my friends hardly recognized me, even by sight. My disposition changed that much."

Roberto may have thought he was relating that experience to confirm what I'd shared with the audience. In reality, the Holy Spirit was using his testimony to rebuke me. I'd often been robbed of joy because I stood stubbornly on some small principle, holding my ground so tenaciously I couldn't see straight.

Know what I did that afternoon? I traded in some *I'm right* strongholds in my life for *I'm not sweating it anymore.*

"Lord," I promised, "from this moment on I'm giving You my right to be right."

Guess what I rediscovered? Joy! I was reminded that the exchange principle I'd been sharing with audiences really works. I just had to get *out of my own way* and do it.

---

### Jehoshaphat Found Joy by Praising God in the Face of Impossibilities.

Some men came and told Jehoshaphat, "A vast army is coming against you from Edom, from the other side of the Sea. . . ."

. . . After consulting the people, Jehoshaphat appointed men to sing to the LORD and to praise him for the splendor of his holiness as they went out at the head of the army, saying: "Give thanks to the LORD, for his love endures forever." As they began to sing and praise, the LORD set ambushes against the men of Ammon and Moab and Mount Seir who were invading Judah, and they were defeated. (*2 Chronicles* 20:2, 21–22)

**Bible Character Joy Lesson #13**

---

Is the right to be right robbing you of joy? Trade it in.

Is uncertain health robbing you of joy? Trade it in.

Are you continually fretting over your future? You wonder if you're ever going to get married or reach your goals? Trade it in!

Perhaps you've always struggled with poor self-image. Trade it in for God's guarantee: "If God is for us, who can be against us? He who did not spare his own Son, but gave him up for us all—how will he not also, along with him, graciously give us all things?" (Romans 8:31–32).

*When we treat people with kindness, the*
*blessings always come back around,*
*and often in unexpected ways.*

The exchange principle does not mean, however, that we just sit down and wait for God to move us. It does not cancel our responsibility to discipline ourselves.

Now every athlete who goes into training conducts himself temperately and restricts himself in all things. They do it to win a wreath that will soon wither, but we [do it to receive a crown of eternal blessedness] that cannot wither. Therefore I do not run uncertainly— without definite aim. I do not box as one beating the air and striking without an adversary. (1 Corinthians 9:25–26 AMPLIFIED)

Perhaps the toughest area to exchange is people-hurts. But even that is possible! How? Make it a habit to live by this directive: "Do nothing out of selfish ambition or vain conceit, but in humility consider others *better* than your-selves" (Philippians 2:3, italics added).

When we treat people with kindness, the blessings al-ways come back around, and often in unexpected ways. Happy and eternally rewarded is the person who learns the fine art of treating other human beings as more important than himself. "Love is patient, love is kind. It does not envy, it does not boast, it is not proud. It is not rude, it is not self-seeking, it is not easily angered, it keeps no record of wrongs" (1 Corinthians 13:4–5).

## SOME KIND OF AN OFFER!

Now for some soothing medicine. We've talked about this exchange process and how tough it can be to carry out. In fact, it is impossible, except God promises to help us. "So I pray for you Gentiles that God who gives you hope will keep you *happy and full of peace* as you believe in him. I pray that God will help you overflow with hope in him through the Holy Spirit's power within you" (Romans 15:13 TLB, italics added).

Remember my valiant Valiant? I'll bet you wonder what ever happened to it. Did the army buy it to demonstrate toughness? Nope. Did a demolition derby driver pay a thousand dollars to crash it on Saturday nights? It was way too dear to me to let it die that way.

Imagine I got a call from the president of the BMW Corporation. "Dale, I've seen you driving that old Plymouth Valiant up and down the street. I've got a special offer for you. The offer is good today, tomorrow, and for the rest of your life. You bring me the keys to your old car, and I will give you keys to a brand-new fifty-thousand-dollar BMW. Straight trade—no money needed."

Some kind of offer, don't you think? That didn't happen. But the universal owner of BMW (Blessings Multiplied Worldwide), *your heavenly Father,* is making that very offer to you spiritually. You give Him the keys to the most miserable part of your life, and He'll give you the keys to kingdom living. The worst of you for the best of Him!

"Dale, you just don't know how discouraged I am," you may be saying. "You don't know how many times I've tried. I've gone to God's throne so many times and come away still clutching my troubles. I just seem to be powerless to exchange my discouragement and heartaches for His joy."

I do know how you feel. I've spent many a day, week, month, and year in that same boat. There have been plenty

of times in my life when I thought feeling defeated must be
the norm, the way I was destined to go through life.

Or maybe you're asking, "What about something I can't
trade in? Something I'm stuck with for life?"

My answer is, park it. Park it at the throne of grace.
Here's what I mean.

Can you imagine what it would feel like to have a giant
set of pliers clamp onto the inside of you, twist three or four
rotations and then hold you in that excruciating position? I
can. When my kidneys go haywire—sometimes for several
days—that's exactly how it feels. Every cell in me that's designed to register pain is jumping up and down and shouting, "Ouch! Ouch! Ouch! Stop, please, stop! I beg you,
stop!"

Could that pain be exchanged for "Wow, what a great
day?"

Maybe not. Not unless God intervenes. And He's very
capable of doing it.

But even if He doesn't, I can take that pain to God's
throne of grace and park myself there. "Lord, I know You
bore the sin and the pain of mankind. You know the pain I'm
feeling. I'm just going to stay right here at the place where
You dispense grace and get every helping of it You'll give
me."

At times, there is no explanation, no answer to our
"Why God?" But I know we have supernatural help.

> For though we live in the world, we do not wage war
> as the world does. The weapons we fight with are not
> the weapons of the world. On the contrary, they have
> divine power to demolish strongholds. We demolish ar-
> guments and every pretension that sets itself up against
> the knowledge of God, and we take captive every
> thought to make it obedient to Christ. (2 Corinthians
> 10:3–5)

You may wonder, "How many times a day do I have to cast down those thoughts, those imaginations that are trying to convince me I'm a joyless Christian and a lifetime loser?"

As often as those negative thoughts come, you fight back in the grace of God! When imaginations come, kick them out in the name of Jesus. When thoughts haunt you, blot them out by the power of His blood. When worry grips you, give it—and keep giving it—to the God who is able to handle any impossibility. Do these things with a feisty persistence that refuses to quit!

Jesus didn't just teach us about prayer, He instructed us how to be persistent in it. "But I'll tell you this—though he won't do it as a friend, if you keep knocking long enough he will get up and give you everything you want—just because of your persistence. And so it is with prayer—keep on asking and you will keep on getting" (Luke 11:8–9 TLB).

God isn't going to give up on you (see 1 Corinthians 1:8–9; Philippians 1:6; 2:12–13; 1 Thessalonians 3:13; 5:23–24; 1 Peter 5:10). *So don't you give up on Him!*

His grace will be there for you tomorrow, and the next day, and the next. Every day until you are home in glory, His grace will be there for you. Keep believing that. Keep on taking the worst part of your life to His throne. Don't stop asking Him to exchange that big-ugly for His awesome joy.

## BIGGIE OR SMALLIE

My daughter Julia came to me discouraged. "Dad, some days I just let everything and everyone drive me crazy. Then I get frustrated with myself for letting stuff get to me, and that makes me even more miserable."

We talked about the principle of exchange. "Take each irritation to God's grace-throne, Julia, and trade it in for a positive, uplifting mind-set."

"I try, Dad. I really do. But you know I'm a perfectionist. Things get to me before I even have any notion that they're coming at me. I don't know if I can change."

"No, you can't. But the Spirit who lives in you is greater than the emotions that live in you. James 1:5 says that you can ask God for wisdom. Ask for as much of it as you want as often as you want. Start each day asking God to help you discern negative imaginations the moment they start incubating in your mind. Then say, 'Imagination, you have no dominion over me. I cast you down in the name of the Lord Jesus Christ.'"

"But they come back," she moaned.

"You're not in a skirmish. You're in a war. So fight."

"How do I know what's to be kicked out and what's OK?"

"It's the biggies versus the smallies," I answered. "Out of fifty instances that could irritate or upset you in a given day, how many are actually critical life issues?"

"Probably about one," she replied sheepishly.

"So, most of the things that haunt you are not biggies. It's the smallies that are getting to you. Right?"

"Right."

"Start asking for God's wisdom to catch those imaginations. Identify them and say, 'You irritating, dingbat smallies, I'm not going to let you ruin my disposition today. Get out. And if you dare come back, by God's power I'm going to kick you out again. And again. And again.'"

Julia had recovered from a frightening eating disorder she'd struggled with in high school and early college. I reminded her, "When you got victory over bulimia, you fought for your life, didn't you? And your attitude toward food changed, didn't it?"

"Of course, Dad," she said.

"With the same persistence you used to fight for your

life, change your outlook on the fears and worries that
plague you. Kick the smallies out of your life, and they will
gradually stop bothering you. They'll eventually get tired of
being thrown out on the street!"

Julia gave me a quick smile and a big hug. She agreed to
start her own "kick out the smallies" campaign and asked me
to remind her of that commitment regularly. I asked her to
do likewise for me.

Imagine my driving into a BMW dealership in that old,
beat-up Valiant and getting a free exchange—my Valiant
for a brand-new BMW. That would be a pretty miraculous
deal! (By the way, I sold that old warrior for three hundred
dollars, and I'll bet it's still running today.)

You can do exactly that spiritually. You are eligible today and every day of your Christian life to exchange your
worst for His best. The circumstances of your life might not
change. But something else will—your attitude!

Trade it in! Your beat-up, ugly-acting temperament for a
brand-new outlook on life. Here's what you count on and
act upon:

> Therefore, since we have a great high priest who has
> gone through the heavens, Jesus the Son of God, let us
> hold firmly to the faith we profess. For we do not have a
> high priest who is unable to sympathize with our weak-
> nesses, but we have one who has been tempted in every
> way, just as we are—yet was without sin. Let us then ap-
> proach the throne of grace with confidence, so that we
> may receive mercy and find grace to help us in our time
> of need. (Hebrews 4:14–16)

You have the invitation to go to God's throne, so go to
it!

Take that hurt, that money problem, that low self-esteem,
that unhappiness, that loneliness to God's throne and do

business with Him. He will give you all the grace, all the help, and all the emotional strength you need—not only to make it through your struggles but even to smile at them.

"I've already failed too many times," you are moaning. "Even if God's not out of grace, He's surely out of patience. I'm just destined for unhappiness."

That's one faithless imagination. *Get rid of it!* Determine by His might to keep on kicking it out of your mind every time it surfaces, no matter how strong or persistent it may seem to be. Consider again the guidelines for God's victory over despair:

> For the weapons of our warfare are not physical (weapons of flesh and blood), but they are mighty before God for the overthrow and destruction of strongholds, [inasmuch as we] refute arguments and theories and reasonings and every proud and lofty thing that sets itself up against the (true) knowledge of God; and we lead every thought and purpose away *captive into the obedience of Christ* the Messiah, the Anointed One. (2 Corinthians 10:4–5 AMPLIFIED, italics added)

When negative thoughts surface, immediately ask for grace. Exchange your weakness for His strength. Repeat the process as often as you need to—even if it's dozens of times a day.

Paul, and thousands of other Christians who have gone before, successfully practiced the trade-it-in principle. You can, too! Don't put it off any longer.

From a dark, dreary dungeon, the fiery apostle exclaimed, "I know what it is to be in need, and I know what it is to have plenty. I have learned the secret of being content in any and every situation, whether well fed or hungry, whether living in plenty or in want. I can do everything through him who gives me strength" (Philippians 4:12–13). *And so can you.*

Therefore, since we are surrounded by such a great cloud of witnesses, let us throw off everything that hinders and the sin that so easily entangles, and let us run with perseverance the race marked out for us. Let us fix our eyes on Jesus, the author and perfecter of our faith, who for the joy set before him endured the cross, scorning its shame, and sat down at the right hand of the throne of God. Consider him who endured such opposition from sinful men, so that you will not grow weary and lose heart. (Hebrews 12:1–3)

# 8

# Critically Contagious

*T*he instant I pushed the last button, I realized I'd dialed the wrong number. Quickly, I hung up so I wouldn't inconvenience anyone. I'd been on the phone for about two hours, returning calls off the answering machine.

I noticed the same name appearing repeatedly on the caller ID. I didn't recognize the name, but he was so persistent I thought it might be important. So I checked my voice mail a couple of times, but there were no messages.

As soon as I'd finished my calls, the phone rang again.

"This is Michael Fowler," he shouted. Using considerable profanity throughout, he asked what business I had dialing his number. He continued without giving me time to reply. "It's unlisted so I won't be bothered by jerks like you."

"I'm so sorry," I replied. "I misdialed and hung up so I wouldn't bother anybody unnecessarily."

He didn't miss a beat. "Sure, and it's people like you who mess up life for people like me. I'm sick and tired of you jerks."

I didn't say what first came to my mind, but when he took a breath I asked, "Did you have a tough day at work?"

"What is that to you?"

*Dale,* I challenged myself, *I dare you to find a way to encourage this man.* I gave it my best shot. "I'm a minister, Michael, and I want you to know that God loves you."

Silence. I waited.

"That's easy for you to say," he finally replied. "You don't have to put up with the garbage I put up with."

"That doesn't change how much God loves either one of us," I answered.

He seemed to get nervous. "I've got to go."

"God loves you," I sneaked in as he hung up.

Michael was more frustrated than the average person—maybe. He'd been just looking for someplace to vent his frustrations. As I talked to him, I couldn't help but wonder what his life could become.

What miracle could occur if he got stuck working around several upbeat, smiling Christians? Might they affect his outlook on life? Could his embittered disposition be transformed if he asked Christ to be his personal Savior?

Yes! A revolutionary process would incubate in Michael's heart. That bitterness would begin to be transformed into joy. The God who forgave Michael would instigate miraculous changes in his disposition. Michael would not only be a new creation in Christ, he'd have access to God's unlimited supply of lovingkindness.

## MELANCHOLY NATION

Michael isn't the only person down in the dumps. I was stunned by a March 8, 1999, article in *U.S. News and World Report* entitled, "Melancholy Nation." Eighteen million Americans are said to be medically depressed. Many more millions are taking medication to alleviate discouragement, pressure, or whatever you might want to call a despondent spirit. Our society is in an epidemic of sorrow.

Surprisingly, less than a million of that 18 million are considered clinically depressed. That means over 17 million people in our country go to school, church, and work in a depressed state every day. And millions more are medically on the borderline of depression.

We Christians are the light of the world for good reason!

There are people in your life today who cannot hide their struggle with this national plague. Others have become good at masking their heavy hearts. Is the joy of the Lord the answer for people around us? *Absolutely.* Medication may help in some instances. Therapy may contribute to healing. But nothing will provide inner strength like Holy Spirit–brought joy.

You don't need a degree in psychotherapy to radiate Christ—to become a genuinely loving encourager. Just be available for God's Spirit to shine through you and give you a heart like this: "We know what real love is from Christ's example in dying for us. And so we also ought to lay down our lives for our Christian brothers. . . . Little children, let us stop just *saying* we love people; let us *really* love them, and *show it* by our *actions*" (1 John 3:16, 18 TLB, italics added).

## WANTED: CONTAGIOUS CHRISTIANS

Michael and many more like him desperately need somebody to remind them what fun feels like. Someone like Scott.

Somehow along life's path, Scott got the idea that life was meant to be enjoyed. After retiring from a career as a commercial pilot, he got another brainstorm. More time available would mean more time to enjoy life!

Scott worked in the youth ministry at our church. Our

youngest daughter, Natalie, our youth director, had to occasionally remind Scott that he was one of the *adults*. Scott was contagious. Sometimes a little crazy, but always contagious.

Once, he decided to toilet-paper-roll our yard as well as Natalie's. What no-rolls-barred works of art!

We retaliated a few weeks later with a 1:00 A.M. phone call from the police—or so we pretended—informing Scott that his neighbors had complained of loud noises and bright lights in his yard. Actually, it was the Crawshaws in his backyard, calling from a cell phone and about to start a big fireworks show. But his dogs and my unconvincing impersonation gave us away. Scott and his family ended up helping us light the fireworks.

Scott returned the favor a few weeks later with a snake in the ice cooler at a youth meeting, and then Natalie countered with a slimy, dead fish under the front seat of his van. That was a good one. The smell lingered for weeks!

Not to be out-pranked, Scott spotted a dead raccoon beside the road. *Gotta find a way to put that poor fella to good use,* he thought. He sneaked around behind Natalie's car and used a long leash to tie the stinky raccoon to the back bumper. Later, on the freeway in pitch darkness, Natalie felt a bump. "Uh-oh," she thought, "I must have a flat."

Another motorist pulled over just as she did, his emergency lights flashing. He approached her car, pale and out of breath. With a quavery voice, he asked, "Ma'am, did you forget you had your pet on a leash tied to your bumper?"

When Natalie saw the raccoon, she had no trouble guessing how it got there. After she had explained the prank war to the helpful motorist, he took the animal, desperately in need of a proper burial, and respectfully laid it to rest in the woods. Natalie began to plot her stage-four counterattack.

Can you imagine a pastor and other church leaders acting so immaturely? There's more to us than pranks and fun.

We put far greater energy and enthusiasm into ministry. But I figure a little laughter and craziness can't hurt. Today's world is so sad, so serious, so joy-starved, people are just plain desperate to discover how to really live. Perhaps it needs people like us to provide a glimpse of the possibility that the Christian life can really be a lot of fun.

*You carry a glorious spiritual virus inside
you—one that everybody around
you needs to catch.*

"I'm really not good for much," Scott sighed to me at a youth retreat he was chaperoning, "except to stir things up now and then."

"Wrong!" I exclaimed. "The time, the encouragement, and even the fun you invest in others' lives are what kingdom-building is all about. People like you are vital to the health of the body of Christ. We need to see people tasting the joy of the Lord so it will become irresistible to us. Keep *showing* us that God and His creation are to be thoroughly enjoyed."

Whether you know it or not, *you* are contagious. You carry a glorious spiritual virus inside you—one that everybody around you needs to catch. It will not only kill the sin-penalty problem they face, it'll make them alive in Christ! "Therefore, there is now no condemnation for those who are in Christ Jesus, because through Christ Jesus the law of the Spirit of life set me free from the law of sin and death" (Romans 8:1–2).

What a way to wake up every day—freed from the law of sin and death! What a motivation to walk above the hassles of life! What an impetus to joyfully take the joy virus everywhere. Let's get to work and spread this wonderful Christianity that can bring joy to a downcast world.

## The Delivered Demoniac Found Joy by Telling of Christ's Majesty.

As Jesus was getting into the boat, the man who had been demon-possessed begged to go with him. Jesus did not let him, but said, "Go home to your family and tell them how much the Lord has done for you, and how he has had mercy on you." So the man went away and began to tell in the Decapolis how much Jesus had done for him. And all the people were amazed. (Mark 5:18–20)

**Bible Character Joy Lesson #14**

The contagious Christianity of the early church is not extinct.

The first believers were awestruck by the many miraculous things done by the Lord and His disciples. Every day they worshiped in the temple courts and had fellowship together in each other's homes. What an irresistible joy they had. Many folks were coming to Christ daily. Their love for the Lord and each other was so strong that many of them sold their possessions to give to ministry and benevolent needs (see Acts 2:42–47).

Joy is our I.D. card. In our sad society, joy sticks out like a sore thumb and draws folks to discover the source, the Lord Jesus Christ.

It's time for us to get out of the Christian Secret Service. Shine, baby, shine!

## AN ATTITUDE OF GRATITUDE

During my years in the construction business, I usually had a couple of employees with sour attitudes that seemed to infect the whole crew. But I had one employee whose positive attitude never ceased to amaze me. Dunk was in his early seventies when he worked as a painter for my company. Many days, when I'd arrive I'd see him on a ladder, singing robustly, going about his work. I remember standing on the ground listening to him sing, shaking my head in amazement. How could someone be that happy fifteen feet off the ground, tediously painting window frames?

When payday came, Dunk would total his hours and round them to the lesser number—after which I'd round them to the higher number. Next, he would tell me what a huge favor I was doing for him to give him a paycheck.

"Dunk, you probably worked three or four hours more than you turned in," I'd say. "You drove your car all over the place to buy materials. I'm the one who should be thanking you."

"Now, Buddy," he'd say, "I know money is hard to come by. I just want you to know how grateful I am for this paycheck. I appreciate what a special employer you are."

What a grateful and joy-filled spirit that man had. He knew how to trade in his worst for God's best. He knew how to get seated in the heavenlies—and stay there the whole day.

Suddenly, Dunk was stricken with a terminal brain tumor. I went to visit him at least once a week during the fifteen months he fought that monster. He would spend the first ten minutes of each visit thanking me for coming. The tumor was inoperable, and he knew he was going to die, but he was still full of gratitude. He'd invariably say, "I know you're busy, Buddy. I just can't get over your coming to see me."

I'd feel so ashamed for letting my small problems get to me.

Usually, I'd share my Sunday morning sermon with Dunk and his wife, Maudie. Whenever I stood to leave, it would take another ten minutes to get out the door because he would shower me with more compliments. "Oh! What a blessing. What a blessing you are to come spend time with us. I'm just so grateful for your good ministry."

The last months of his life, he barely had the strength to speak. But still he'd whisper, "Thank you for taking the time to come, Buddy. You're such a joy to me."

Here was a man literally on his deathbed and in a great deal of discomfort, yet he remained full of appreciation. He lived a rich life because he was a genuinely grateful person. He died a noble death for the same reason.

Without a thankful spirit, we miss out on thousands of hours of joy. We get stuck in a miserable trap of ungratefulness. Today is the day to begin ripping away the tentacles of ingratitude. It's time to cultivate an attitude of gratitude. Anyone can do it. "Speak to one another with psalms, hymns and spiritual songs. Sing and make music in your heart to the Lord, always giving thanks to God the Father for everything, in the name of our Lord Jesus Christ" (Ephesians 5:19–20).

This attitude of gratitude only thrives when I take the time to renew my mind through meditating on God's Word. Psalm 119:130 says, "The unfolding of your words gives light; it gives understanding to the simple." I believe this light is both spiritual *and* physical. As His Word saturates our heart, our inner man becomes literally illuminated. That's when we begin to glow from the inside out. Like Dunk did. A glow that others can actually see and feel.

*You can be the one-in-a-thousand person*
*who is consistently joyful.*

Soak in the promises of God's Word. Then have the time of your life radiating the joy of those promises to everyone in sight! Like Dunk, you'll be was gloriously contagious.

How do I become contagious? If I'm going to have a positive impact on the lives of people around me, they must see something opposite the negativity they expect in others. They need to see something to make them want Jesus. Even my fellow Christians need to see something different in me. They need to see me walking in joy.

That visible joy will be a wake-up call to others. It will be a jump-start for fellow Christians to come out of their stale, stalled state and start growing spiritually once again. "It gave me great joy to have some brothers come and *tell about your faithfulness* to the truth and how you continue to walk in the truth" (3 John 3, italics added).

You can be the one-in-a-thousand person who is consistently joyful. You'll not only fuel your own fire, you'll warm the hearts of people around you.

My son Ben learned this firsthand during his sophomore year in college. He had transferred to a school eight hours from home to play baseball in a program that had produced a number of pro ballplayers.

At first, he felt totally lost and lonely. He knew absolutely no one at the school, and it only got worse when he did get to know some of them. His three roommates stayed up half the night doing crazy things, and he had no Christian fellowship.

His coaches seemed like psychos. They cursed often, lost what self-control they had during games, and often threw bats out of the dugout onto the field. One time the head coach got so furious at an umpire's call that he stormed out onto the field and sat Indian-style with his back to the ump. He refused to move, so the umpire ordered his players to carry him off the field!

Ben called home late one night. "Dad," he said, "I'm really

hurting. No, make that, I'm dying. I've got to find some Christian friends. I just don't think I can go on."

Like any dad, I felt like saying, "C'mon home, Son." I wanted to, but I didn't.

"Ben," I said, "I think you need to start blessing people. You need to start rubbing off on some of those guys."

"But, Dad, I'm desperate," he begged. "I'm calling for help."

"I know, Son. That's why I'm telling you to start blessing people. Pick out at least one person each day and bless him. Verbally or nonverbally, find a way to uplift him right where he is in his life. Spread some joy."

Ben was quiet, apparently considering what I'd said. "Jesus promised in Matthew 10:39," I continued, "that 'whoever finds his life will lose it, and whoever loses his life for my sake will find it.' Start losing your life in others, Son, and I guarantee you'll discover joy and happiness you never dreamed possible."

Well, Ben had heard that before, and he believed in the principle. This was the acid test. He'd be the first to tell you he struggled painfully with the idea. But he stuck with it. He started seeking people out and asking God for wisdom to find a way to bless them.

A few weeks later, he started a Bible study with a group of guys, all but one being non-Christians. Small miracles—if there is such a thing as a small one—began on that campus.

When I visited him that spring, he greeted me with a smile from ear to ear. "Dad, it works, it really works!" he nearly shouted. "What you give up by giving your life away is nothing compared to what God gives back!"

## LIVE IT—LOVE IT—SHARE IT

Are you contagious?

It's been said that you're the best Christian somebody knows. That's true of almost any Christian. In fact, you may be the *only* Christian somebody knows.

Joy, and the fire that comes with it, make you a unique person in today's society. You'll have a dynamic message to share with people around you even when you're not saying a word. A person who is vibrant and full of joy simply cannot be ignored. I don't know about you, but I want to be that kind of person.

Here's the bottom line: Know who you are in Christ. Live it. Love it. Share it. Be bold. The Lord your God is with you! Joy always spawns more joy. As you *radiate* joy, you'll be the *recipient* of more joy than you ever imagined!

Driving down the highway, I passed a gray-haired gentleman looking under the hood of an old truck stalled on the side of the road. My mechanical skills test out at below zero, so I knew I'd be no help with the engine. But I decided to stop anyway. He was a captive audience to hear the gospel!

"Thirty years ago, I blew a chance to become a Christian," he moaned, "and God's been punishing me ever since. I'm unforgivable."

"What do you think the Bible means when it says, 'God is love?'" I asked.

He said nothing.

"What about John 3:16? 'For God so loved the world that he gave his one and only Son, that whoever believes in him shall not perish but have eternal life.'"

"I missed my chance," he said with grief. "I missed my chance."

I smiled. "Why don't you bow your head and pray with me right now, right here beside this busy road? Why don't you get this settled forever? Why not acknowledge God as He really is—One who loves you inexpressibly and longs to forgive you?"

He was so close to doing just that, but he didn't. He was that convinced he was unforgivable.

Did I drive away defeated and joyless? Absolutely not! I

was disappointed, but at the same time, I was rejoicing that I had shared God's love and forgiveness. It's an uplifting experience to tell the gospel story, whether your testimony is received or rejected. It's exhilarating to brag about the goodness of God. So start bragging!

On the contrary, we speak as men approved by God to be entrusted with the gospel. We are not trying to please men but God, who tests our hearts.

. . . For what is our hope, our joy, or the crown in which we will glory in the presence of our Lord Jesus when he comes? Is it not you? Indeed, you are our glory and joy. (1 Thessalonians 2:4, 19–20)

---

## Jonah Lost the Joy of Ministry by Being Preoccupied with Himself.

When the sun rose, God provided a scorching east wind, and the sun blazed on Jonah's head so that he grew faint. He wanted to die, and said, "It would be better for me to die than to live."

But God said to Jonah, "Do you have a right to be angry about the vine?"

"I do," he said. "I am angry enough to die."

But the LORD said, "You have been concerned about this vine, though you did not tend it or make it grow. It sprang up overnight and died overnight. But Nineveh has more than a hundred and twenty thousand people who cannot tell their right hand from their left, and many cattle as well. Should I not be concerned about that great city?" (Jonah 4:8–11)

**Bible Character Joy Lesson #15**

---

## JOY HERITAGE

In my first pastorate, a semiretired gentleman named Bert attended the church. Bert was personable, knowledgeable about the Bible, and well respected in the congregation. He'd attended for nearly two years when he came to me one day.

"There's not enough emphasis on sharing Christ with nonbelievers here," he said. His countenance and disposition revealed a judgmental spirit, and it was starting to rub off on others in the fellowship.

I knew Bert had a good heart, and I tried to handle his feelings with respect. "Bert, I'll come to your house every Tuesday night at seven-thirty," I suggested. "We'll go out together in your subdivision and knock on doors. We'll share Christ with everyone who'll come to the door."

He agreed.

We did that the following two Tuesdays. The third Tuesday, when I arrived, he said something had come up and he could not go, so I went by myself. Not long afterward, he lost interest entirely.

For a few months, Bert backed off from criticizing; then back he came like gangbusters, unhappy about something else. You can't escape the fruit of a judgmental spirit for long. After a while, his sour outlook began to cause division within the church.

*Call back to us and shout, "Rest in Him.*
*He is faithful. He will never leave*
*you nor forsake you."*

In time, Bert left the church. But a dampening effect had taken hold of the enthusiasm level of the other folks. It took weeks to restore a positive spirit in our little church.

That dear, gray-haired man could have had such a powerful positive impact on our church. He could have injected a spirit of joy and optimism into young families watching his example. But he chose not to be that person.

I have something to say to you folks nearing or in your retirement years. I know there are a lot of things about life, about health, about money, and even about people that can be very discouraging. The pressures of a world literally going crazy can be exasperating and sometimes frightening.

All of us who are younger desperately need your joy and optimism. We need you to pass along hope to us by your life and your example. Oh, how we need your words to assure us that all things really do work together for good to those who love God. You are uniquely qualified to say that, since you've experienced it. You've lived out the reality that God is a loving and faithful Father.

Call back to us and shout, "Rest in Him. He is faithful. He will never leave you nor forsake you. Don't be discouraged. Let the joy of the Lord be your strength!"

After forty-two years of missionary work my father-in-law, Pop Elbe, retired for health reasons. Parkinson's disease slowed the once-robust man to a snail's pace.

Some days, it was quite an effort for him to make his face smile the smile in his heart. But smile he did. He just kept right on ministering, though in slow motion.

Every third Sunday, Rev. Elbe spoke to our congregation. We would prop him behind a table next to the pulpit and then listen, spellbound, as he taught the Scriptures from his vast knowledge and experience. Though his voice was barely a whisper, the radiance on his face moved us as he shared how he had learned—even as he had traveled worldwide in ministry—that God is faithful.

Pop never missed a church service or function. Every time I made a hospital visit as a pastor, he was there with me. I'd push him in his wheelchair right up to a hospital bed, and he'd whisper words of hope, sprinkled with a joke or two. Often, doctors and nurses would stop what they were doing to absorb his glow and his wisdom.

Spreading joy was so much a part of Pop Elbe's nature that old age, pain, slurred speech, and having to be propped up in his wheelchair couldn't put out his fire.

You might be thinking, *Well, that was probably just his nature. He must have been one of those people born smiling.*

I've heard otherwise. I'm told he grew up in an immigrant family that was not at all demonstrative. He had a difficult childhood and knew tragedy well. But when he found Christ as a young adult, he also discovered joy, and he simply refused to go through life without it.

Pop proved to me that a person can taste joy in good times and in trying ones too. And his witness brought many others to joyful living along the way.

I don't know about you, but if I'm someday known as a person who spent a lifetime spreading joy, I'll consider my life very, very rich.

You don't have to be retired from the mission field to tell others about God's ways. Whatever your background or position in life, you have something to share. Spread a spirit of joy. Your life is far more valuable than you imagine, and your ministry can be richer than you may have realized.

Why? Because you've been where we younger folks are headed. And if you can assure us, "God's grace is sufficient to give you joy all the way," imagine what that would mean to us.

You may have reasoned, "People just don't care to hear from the older generation anymore. There's not much of a place for people like me in the church today." Wrong. *We need you!* Give us a smile and a countenance that says, "It will be worth it all when we see Jesus," and you'll be astounded at how vital your ministry will be.

Whether you're young or old, a new believer or someone

many years in the faith, you are a significant influence on others. There is a joy virus to be spread everywhere. To everyone. Every day. You'd probably be astounded if you knew how your smile and optimism would touch the hearts of your brothers and sisters in Christ—even those you think have their act together.

---

### Barnabas Found Joy by Encouraging Others to Stand Firm in Their Faith.

News of this reached the ears of the church at Jerusalem, and they sent Barnabas to Antioch. When he arrived and saw the evidence of the grace of God, he was glad and encouraged them all to remain true to the Lord with all their hearts. He was a good man, full of the Holy Spirit and faith, and a great number of people were brought to the Lord. (*Acts 11:22–24*)

**Bible Character Joy Lesson #16**

---

Three vital thoughts about the positive impact of our joy upon others jump out of the wisdom of Proverbs.

Joy Affects Family Relationships

"A wise son brings joy to his father, but a foolish man despises his mother" (Proverbs 15:20).

"If someone else in this family would show some genuine happiness," you might say, "I'd give it a try myself." Wrong approach. *You* lead the way. You be the person who has such a walk with the Lord that joy radiates from you.

I've seen a bumper sticker that reads, "If Mama ain't happy, ain't nobody happy!" There's a lot of truth in that. But you can change it to, "If Sonny's happy, you'll catch some, too." Your joy *can* and *will* be contagious in your family.

You might be in a blues family, one that seems energized not by enjoying one another, but by arguing with one another. All the more reason to ask God to fill you with joy, then patiently watch the miraculous changes in your family. Even if those changes take years, look what you've enjoyed all that time you've been waiting: gladness of heart!

## Joy Changes the Hearts and Health of People Around Us

"A cheerful look brings joy to the heart, and good news gives health to the bones" (Proverbs 15:30).

How amazingly our countenance affects people around us—even people we meet on the street!

Think about it. Your joy, and the encouraging words that accompany it, can even aid someone's physical healing!

The opposite of a cheerful look is a scowl. Ever met a scowler? That's what I call a Christian who's so intense, so serious, so overwhelmed by life that he can't even muster a smile.

If the scowler happens to sit in the middle of the audience at church, it's a difficult sight for a pastor. Try as he might, a scowler's frowning can hardly be ignored as the pastor tries to uplift the congregation. He's preaching his heart out, and there's the scowler challenging every word with his countenance.

I've learned an important lesson from the scowlers I've encountered. It's this: Even one person can drastically affect the temperature of an entire group. Positively or negatively, we impact other people simply by our countenance.

Something that amazes me about scowlers is that when everyone else is laughing, they scowl all the more tenaciously. It bothers them when other people enjoy the Lord and each other.

Don't be a scowler. Read this book as many times as you need to. Look up and meditate on every verse listed. Study your Bible diligently for more uplifting promises. Replace that defeatism with a whole new you. Hang around God-omistic people. Get unstuck from the muck. Start wearing a smile and acting like the zillionaire child of the King you are.

Since you're going to affect the spiritual temperature around you, make sure you cause it to rise, not fall. Be a joy to your pastor, your teachers, and everyone around you who is working to further God's kingdom. Hebrews 13:17 says, "Obey your leaders and submit to their authority. They keep watch over you as men who must give an account. Obey them so that their work will be a joy, not a burden, for that would be of no advantage to you."

Let's say, "Lord, I admit that many of the circumstances in life really can't be changed. Give me the wisdom to ac-knowledge James 4:6 and other Scriptures that promise Your grace. Give me an abundance of that grace to push aside this impatience, this intolerance, and this impetuous-ness so I might become a more joyful person. I need a mega-dose of heaven-brought joy to keep me out of the rut of discouragement and so full of You I could glow in the dark."

That's the kind of disposition God will use to change people's hearts—and even their health.

Joy Builds Strong Friendships

"Perfume and incense bring joy to the heart, and the pleasantness of one's friend springs from his earnest counsel" (Proverbs 27:9).

Just as the physical senses can receive joy from "God, who richly provides us with everything for our enjoyment" (1 Timothy 6:17), so joy also comes from the uplifting spirit of a friend.

### None of our sorrows is wasted in God's economy.

God designed us to receive joy from others. Family and friends, especially those growing in Christ, are a unique safety net for us. Those feelings of security, in themselves, bring much joy.

We're not in this thing just for ourselves. "Iron sharpeneth iron; so a man sharpeneth the countenance of his friend" (Proverbs 27:17 KJV). That shows how much we rub off on each other. How we need each other! When a friend comes alongside us in a struggle, it brings added spiritual strength.

Tough things that happen to us and force us to draw closer to God are never wasted.

What a wonderful God we have—he is the Father of our Lord Jesus Christ, the source of every mercy, and the one who so wonderfully comforts and strengthens us in our hardships and trials. And why does he do this? So that when others are troubled, needing our sympathy and encouragement, *we can pass on to them* this same help and comfort God has given us. (2 Corinthians 1:3–4 TLB, italics added)

Wow! None of our sorrows is wasted in God's economy.

While the apostle Paul was ready—even anxious—to leave his earthly body behind and taste heaven, he sensed God saying, "Not yet." The Holy Spirit must have reminded him that while God chooses to leave us on this planet, we're to be critically contagious for Christ—to unbelievers and to fellow Christians.

Paul said, "Convinced of this, I know that I will remain,

and I will continue with all of you for your progress and joy in the faith, so that through my being with you again your joy in Christ Jesus will overflow on account of me" (Philippians 1:25–26).

"You mean, I have the power to cause joy to bubble over in others?" you ask. You bet! The God of all grace living inside you waits to use His power to bless people *through you.* All you have to do is climb off the "I" throne and learn the blessed art of genuinely caring about others.

## GOLF EVANGELISM

I don't recall exactly how Jim and I met. But I do remember his general outlook on life, especially toward people who called themselves Christians.

A former college football star, Jim had married and gotten off to an exceptional start in business. Exceptional, that is, until he signed several marketing contracts with a couple of guys who professed to be Christians.

Misrepresentations and loopholes left Jim holding the bag. He lost his shirt and, with it, any interest in Christianity. He knew just enough about the Bible to hold his ground in any evangelistic appeal tossed his way.

I simply ignored his sarcasm and asked him jokingly if he'd take me golfing sometime.

His response surprised me. "I'd really like to do that, but you have to promise me you won't talk about God."

"OK," I hesitantly agreed, "and you have to promise me you'll stop judging God by the Christians you've done business with."

He cracked a faint smile and hesitantly agreed.

Jim was an excellent golfer. His ball quickly found its way to the first green. Mine had entirely different notions. It seemed magnetically pulled to any and all water, most clumps of trees, and occasionally the wrong fairway.

Jim had promised not to ridicule Christians, but that didn't include falling off the golf cart in hysterics over his Christian friend's clumsy golf antics.

We played weekly for several months. My golf improved a little, so we had to find other things to occupy our conversations.

I took a genuine interest in things he was interested in. But, mostly, I just plain enjoyed life in front of him. Whether golf, or careers, or family, or pro sports was the subject, I found a way to laugh and smile often.

Lo and behold, it started to rub off on him. We were putting out the eighteenth hole of a course we'd often played when he queried, "What makes you enjoy life so much?"

"Hard for me to answer that, Jim, without talking about God."

"OK, I'll give you fifteen minutes," he answered with a grin.

Boy, can I talk fast when I have to.

Jim didn't respond. No words. No expression. Nothing.

*Maybe I talked too fast,* I thought. *Oh well, back to plan A— just live it.*

Months later out of the blue Jim said, "You're bugging me, Dale. You've got something I don't have—something I swore I'd never want. I can argue with your theology, but I'm having an impossible time arguing with your happiness."

This time I said nothing, but my smile must have been jumping right off my face!

A few weeks later, on his own timetable, Jim went for a long walk and had a long talk with God. He prayed, "Lord, I want to be in Your family. Please forgive my sins."

Jim changed. He started glowing. He even began taking business associates to play golf just to tell them about Christ. His God became irresistible to people around him. He became contagious for God to the highest degree—critically contagious.

You and I can be critically contagious, too. We can start spreading joy, and the kingdom of God that generates joy, wherever we go. Let's keep in mind that whatever sacrifice it takes to be a joy spreader is nothing compared to the blessings we receive in return.

From his dungeon office, Paul told us how to become one.

If you have any encouragement from being united with Christ, if any comfort from his love, if any fellowship with the Spirit, if any tenderness and compassion, then make my joy complete by being like-minded, having the same love, being one in spirit and purpose. Do nothing out of selfish ambition or vain conceit, but in humility consider others better than yourselves. Each of you should look not only to your own interests, but also to the interests of others. Your attitude should be the same as that of Christ Jesus. (Philippians 2:1–5)

"Lord, make me a blessing to just one person today."

Can you say that? It will revolutionize your life. I guarantee it.

# Don't Leave Home Without It

If there is such a thing as Murphy's Law, it certainly is creative. I say that from firsthand experience.

I'd just gone through a painful career change. We Crawshaws were packed like sardines into a tiny attic apartment. Things were beginning to literally crack up.

I went downstairs to hunt for something packed in one of the many boxes we were living out of. It was dark, and I couldn't find the light switch. As I headed in the direction I thought I needed to go, I banged into an old glass door. It shattered with the impact, and a huge shard drove deep into my leg just below the kneecap.

Surgery. Recovery. The hindrances of life on crutches. Little insurance. Almost no money. A brand-new part-time ministry position and the politics that accompanied it. Add to the list desertion by a trusted friend. Heart-wrenching criticism from another—the only one left.

I was low. Very low. Joy seemed a million miles away. Debt pressure was piling up. Worst of all, I couldn't afford to act discouraged. What little income we had came from my new job where I was on trial to perform.

Did Murphy have me by the tail? Was the roaring lion, the devil himself, about to devour me? Or was my heavenly Father taking me deeper into Christian maturity?

I wish I could tell you that one bright morning I just snapped out of it. I didn't. But I didn't give up, either. I kept fighting. I refused to give in to thoughts that God no longer cared about me.

I constantly reminded myself of the powerful truth I shared with you earlier:

> For *though we walk [live] in the flesh,* we are *not* carrying on our warfare according to the flesh and *using mere human weapons.* For the weapons of our warfare are not physical (weapons of flesh and blood), but they are *mighty* before God for the overthrow and destruction of strongholds, [inasmuch as we] refute arguments and theories and reasonings and every proud and lofty thing that sets itself up against the (true) knowledge of God; and we lead every thought and purpose away captive into the obedience of Christ the Messiah, the Anointed One. (2 Corinthians 10:3–5 AMPLIFIED, italics added)

I was aware that my emotions were playing tricks on me. My thoughts of defeat became well-documented arguments in private courtroom trials to convince myself I was a loser. If I allowed them to continue, I knew they'd become strongholds—places in my spiritual, emotional, intellectual, and even physical makeup held captive by negative accusations.

I realized that the more strongholds occupied in my mind, the less joy I'd experience. The idea of carrying around monuments to my discouragement repulsed me.

I remember telling myself, *Fight, Dale, fight. Don't give in to these destructive meditations.* After that, whenever negative thoughts came rushing into my mind, I'd talk to them. "In the name of Jesus, I kick you out. You have no place here."

It was often a weary reply, but it was a response, nonetheless.

In that dark time, I held on to the light. "The entrance of thy words giveth light; it giveth understanding unto the simple" (Psalm 119:130 KJV). I believed then, as I believe now, that God's Word brings spiritual, emotional and even physical light—powerful light that combats gloom-and-doom thinking.

While my progress was slow and grudging, it was progress. It is in such dark times that we search our hearts and begin to tear down those strongholds. That must happen for joy to increase.

Journey with me a few more steps. Let's see if we can put the icing on the cake in figuring out *how* to consistently walk in joy.

What if I picked a day, called you up, and asked you, "What are some of the benefits God piled on you today?" Would that catch you off guard?

You might say, "Hey, I'm too full of problems and perplexities to be thinking about benefits." If we could be really honest about it, we get pretty irritated at God sometimes. "Lord, I really don't like what You are allowing to happen to me. Things are too tough. How long are You going to leave me in limbo?"

In that frame of mind, before we know it, weeds of bitterness will spring up and take over our heart. We are given grave warnings about the consequences of idolatry—of serving self or something other than Jehovah. Idolatry always brings bitterness, and bitterness always produces sorrow. "Make sure there is no man or woman, clan or tribe among you today whose heart turns away from the LORD our God to go and worship the gods of those nations; make sure there is no root among you that produces such bitter poison" (Deuteronomy 29:18; see also Ephesians 3:30–31).

## DAILY GARDENING

When I was a kid, I had to learn the splendid art of weed pulling. I hated it! I got a penny a weed, but I didn't care an iota about the money. I'd ask, "Mom, can't I do it next week?"

You know, there's a thing about weeds. The longer you wait, the harder they are to get rid of. If you wait too long, it's like pulling a small tree out of the ground. More than once, I remember thinking, *Uh-oh, I wish I hadn't waited.*

---

### Judas Forfeited Joy by Choosing Not to Live by the Words of Jesus.

Early in the morning, all the chief priests and the elders of the people came to the decision to put Jesus to death. They bound him, led him away and handed him over to Pilate, the governor.

When Judas, who had betrayed him, saw that Jesus was condemned, he was seized with remorse and returned the thirty silver coins to the chief priests and the elders. "I have sinned," he said, "for I have betrayed innocent blood."

"What is that to us?" they replied. "That's your responsibility."

So Judas threw the money into the temple and left. Then he went away and hanged himself. (*Matthew 27:1–5*)

**Bible Character Joy Lesson #17**

---

Every day we face perplexing circumstances, people, problems, and questions about the way God is orchestrating life. If those questions are not answered with "God is sovereign, and He has my best interest at heart," bitter weeds spring up in our hearts. The bigger those weeds get, the less the joy! Why? Because those roots of bitterness ruthlessly gobble up all the nourishment that joy needs to thrive.

We must do our gardening daily—when we feel like it and when we don't.

The problem is, we want to do selective gardening. "Lord, you know that negative thought taking root in the corner of my heart, that one over there? Yes, that one. That one sort of feels good. I deserve to nurse that one along a little bit longer. Could we wait a few weeks before I release ownership of that stronghold-in-the-making? I just really don't want to deal with that one yet."

That's sure disaster. Don't go there! Ask God this moment to do divine surgery wherever bitter roots are growing, even if you have every right to nurse those open wounds.

Joy comes when you and I look at life from a faith-filled perspective and forbid bitterness to take root in our hearts. Refuse the spirit of despair. Over things at school. Over pressures at work. Over someone's words that plastered us to the wall. Even over the injustices of life itself.

I've learned the importance of keeping the garden weeded. When I do, there will be a tenderness in me. The ground in my heart will be fertile. It will grow the best joy I've ever tasted!

After thirty-five years of belonging to God's family, I realize how far I've got to go to become consistently joyful. Many of the giants I once considered overpowering in my life, though, are less intimidating now.

I find myself laughing at things that once ruined my day or my whole week. My vision clears more quickly. I see and

appreciate things that once were smothered by negative attitudes that tried to suffocate my heart. Life's taste buds
work better. I can savor God's presence and life's endow-
ments.

> Send forth your light and your truth,
>     let them guide me;
> let them bring me to your holy mountain,
>     to the place where you dwell.
> Then will I go to the altar of God,
>     to God, my joy and my delight. . . .
> Why are you downcast, O my soul?
>     Why so disturbed within me?
> Put your hope in God,
>     for I will yet praise him,
>     my Savior and my God.
>
> —Psalm 43:3–5

I've heard some heart-wrenching stories about the or-
phanages in Russia and Third World countries. Some of the
children in those institutions were given to the government
simply because they were starving at home. Others were left
as newborns—some in shoeboxes—on the steps of public
buildings. Their parents could not possibly earn enough
money to keep them alive. Many were taken by the state
because of extreme parental alcoholism or abuse.

Those little orphans beam with appreciation for even
the smallest bit of attention. The smiles on their faces blow
you away. Obviously, they have few possessions, but their
most treasured are usually photographs—pictures of anything, anybody, any place.

Why, I wondered? Why would that little face light up
because of a simple photograph? Then it hit me. It represents
a hope, something *outside* the four walls of the orphanage the
child has known all his life.

Can you imagine that? A little face radiant because of the hope represented in a four by five photograph? Do I have the slightest excuse to live in less than abandoned joy and victory?

*Dale, it's time to get out of the "me and mine" rut. You don't need a picture. The blessings surrounding you in abundance are not images, but the real thing. It's time not to only count them but to pass them along by the joy you exhibit to everybody, everywhere, every day.*

*It's time to get out your Bible—your picture of heaven—and start living like someone on a journey to a better place, someone joyfully anticipating what's just ahead.*

But because of his great love for us, God, who is rich in mercy, made us alive with Christ even when we were dead in transgressions—it is by grace you have been saved. And God raised us up with Christ and seated us with him in the heavenly realms in Christ Jesus. (Ephesians 2:4–6)

## CHASED DOWN BY A BLESSING

Dave and I were running late. Literally running and late. We were in St. Louis and heard on the radio that one of the biggest hockey games of the year might not be sold out.

As we dashed through the streets toward the arena, we noticed someone running after us. And it didn't take more than a glance to see he had no dearth of size or strength. *Uh-oh, we're being chased by a mugger,* I thought, *a big, strong one!* We ran faster and faster, but there was no shaking this big fellow.

"Hey, guys, stop," he shouted. "I've got something for you."

*Sure you do,* I thought, *a knife or a gun or a knuckle sandwich.*

I was gasping from the running but even more from the thought of having to defend myself against this huge man.

We put on another burst of speed, but so did he. He caught us just a block from the arena.

### God is giving you daily opportunities to enjoy the best seat in the house.

*This is it,* I told myself. *We're goners.*

"You guys sure know how to run from something good," he panted. We both flinched as he reached into his pocket. Out came, not a knife, not a gun, but two eighty-dollar tickets to the game.

"I can't make the game tonight," he huffed, "and these are at ice level right behind the goalie—the best seats in the house. I couldn't stand to see them wasted. They're yours. Free." He dashed off, leaving us staring at the two tickets. "And thanks for the exercise," he called over his shoulder.

Best seats in the house! Somebody had run us down to make sure we didn't miss out on them. That's exactly what our God is doing. Pursuing us. Looking for every opportunity to demonstrate His goodness to us. He earnestly desires that we taste the joy He's created for us—every day!

In fact, one of His phenomenal attributes is that His goodness and mercy are right in the middle of everything He does. This is mind-boggling to me: The things God decides or does are *filtered through His goodness before they are carried out!* "The Lord is gracious and full of compassion; slow to anger, and of great mercy. The Lord is good to all: and his tender mercies are *over all* his works" (Psalm 145:8–9 KJV, italics added).

Get that? God is giving you daily opportunities to enjoy the best seat in the house—a heavenly viewpoint that prevents you from sweating the small stuff and keeps you really enjoying the big stuff.

I want to live a rich life. Don't you? Here's how to do it:

So ever since we first heard about you we have kept on praying and asking God to help you understand what he wants you to do; . . . asking that the way you live will always please the Lord and honor Him, so that you will always be doing good, kind things for others, while all the time you are learning to know God better and better.

We are praying, too, that you will be filled with His mighty, glorious strength so that you can keep going no matter what happens—always full of the joy of the Lord, and always thankful to the Father who has made us fit to share all the wonderful things that belong to those who live in the Kingdom of light. For He has rescued us out of the darkness and gloom of Satan's kingdom and brought us into the Kingdom of His dear Son, who bought our freedom with His blood and forgave us all our sins. (Colossians 1:10–14 TLB)

If that wouldn't lift you right out of the chair you're sitting in, I don't know what would. You have been rescued—rescued from the darkness and terror of Satan's kingdom. You've been set free by Christ's blood, freed to celebrate all of the wonder and majesty of the life God has given you to experience. Whoa, Baby! What a life.

## HEAVENLY POWER PLANT

I am given the keys to the heavenly power plant inside me. But if I don't know how to turn it on, I miss out on my heavenly seat. And sometimes that's exactly what happens.

Recently, I learned what it's like not to know how to make the connection. I needed to make a phone call. I was standing next to a construction vehicle and noticed the owner had a cellular phone in his truck.

He readily agreed to let me use it. "Take your time,

friend," he said.

I dialed the number and waited. Nothing happened. It was dead.

"Hello— Hello—" I said. No answer.

I dialed again, making sure I included the area code. Dead again.

On the third try, I knew I'd done everything right, but it sure sounded quiet on the other end of the line. "Hello," I said, "is anybody home?"

The construction worker stood a few feet away, watching me out of the corner of his eye. I noticed an amused look on his face.

"There's something wrong with your phone," I called to him.

Without saying a word, he walked over, took the phone out of my hand, turned it around and put it to my ear. Then he winked and walked away. I'd been talking into the wrong side of the phone.

*"God has extra joy for you, to restore—*
*to tenfold restore—the years the*
*disappointments have consumed."*

Just like the power of the company behind that phone, when you become God's child, you instantly become eligible for all of God's promises. Resurrection power is there. In superabundance. All we've got to do is get connected to it.

Remember the guarantee we discussed?

Now we live with a wonderful expectation because Jesus Christ rose again from the dead. For God has reserved a priceless inheritance for his children. It is kept in heaven for you, pure and undefiled, beyond the reach of change and decay. And God, in his mighty power, will protect you until you receive this salvation, because you are trusting him. . . . So be truly glad! There is wonderful joy ahead, even though it is necessary for you to endure many trials for a while. (1 Peter 1:3–6 NLT)

Furthermore, "to all who received him, to those who believed in his name, he gave the right to become children of God" (John 1:12). With that relationship comes a capacity for joy—a joy that is supernatural and unexplainable! It's not just a matter of how I view life. It's who I am that makes joy possible. I've been adopted into God's family. That adoption made me free from sin and death and gave me an out-of-this-world capacity for joy.

After I speak about joy, someone invariably tells me something like this: "My life has been full of rotten circumstances, and the idea of joy is absolutely foreign to me. I've spent so many years without it, there's no way I can start experiencing it now."

Here's the promise of God I point out to them:

Be glad, O people of Zion,
    rejoice in the LORD your God,
for He has given you
    the autumn rains in righteousness.
He sends you abundant showers,
    both autumn and spring rains, as before.
The threshing floors will be filled with grain;
    the vats will overflow with new wine and oil.

I will repay you the years the locusts have eaten—
    the great locust and the young locust,
    the other locusts and the locust swarm—
my great army that I sent among you.
You will have plenty to eat, until you are full,
    and you will praise the name of the LORD your God,

who has worked wonders for you;
never again will my people be shamed.

—Joel 2:23–26

That's the promise we gave our adopted daughter,
Dawn, when she came into the Crawshaw family. "The
empty, joyless years of your past do not dictate your future,"
we assured her. "God has extra joy for you, to restore—to
tenfold restore—the years the disappointments have consumed."

We encouraged her to forget the past and to focus on
what lies ahead (see Philippians 3:13). She is smiling evidence that God can and will do exactly what He promised.

## LIVING WILL

What happens in our hearts when we really grasp how
much we inherited when God adopted us? Freedom! Freedom to partake of the joy of the Lord to full capacity. "May
the God of hope fill you with all joy and peace as you trust
in Him, so that you may overflow with hope by the power
of the Holy Spirit" (Romans 15:13).

"Then I would still have this consolation—*my joy in unrelenting pain*—that I had not denied the words of the Holy
One" (Job 6:10, italics added). If Job could find strength and
joy in the midst of unrelenting pain, then we can find it, too,
in pain or even in the mundane!

Say you were at fault in an auto accident. The judge
awarded a $500,000 settlement to the other party. Your in-
surance will pay only $300,000. You'll owe $200,000! It
would be impossible for you to pay.

Major bummer—*except* that you just got a certified letter
from your millionaire aunt informing you that her living will
has already been signed. It stipulates a transfer of $4.5 mil-
lion into your bank account in exactly twelve months. It's a

done deal. Your bank has already received the paperwork. You're going to get hounded for a while for that $200,000, aren't you? Lawyers will call. Threats will be made. Inconveniences. Hassles, to say the least.

What's on your mind, though? The future. That little $200,000 is nothing compared to the glory of $4.5 million. You can smile at a lot of things when you know what's ahead, can't you?

So start smiling! What's ahead for you is so far beyond your happiest dreams, it makes $4.5 million dollars look like a quarter. "However, as it is written: 'No eye has seen, no ear has heard, no mind has conceived what God has prepared for those who love him'" (1 Corinthians 2:9).

Wow! I'm a spiritual locomotive. An absolute dynamo because He lives in me. "Therefore, my dear brothers, stand firm. Let nothing move you. Always give yourselves fully to the work of the Lord, because you know that your labor in the Lord is not in vain" (1 Corinthians 15:58).

You serve an awesome God. A God who loves you no matter what and who rewards you for obedience to Him. Victory is in walking by faith. It's in claiming His promises, standing on them, and sharing them with others. That faith-walk takes us down the highway of joy—the high road. Remember, "Though you *have not seen him,* you love him; and even though you do not see him now, you believe in him and are filled with an inexpressible and glorious joy" (1 Peter 1:8, italics added).

---

### Joshua Found Joy by Choosing to Serve God Wholeheartedly.

"But if serving the LORD seems undesirable to you, then choose for yourselves this day whom you will serve, whether the gods your forefathers served beyond the River, or the gods of the Amorites, in whose land you are living. But as for me and my household, we will serve the LORD." (*Joshua 24:16*)

**Bible Character Joy Lesson #18**

---

Jesus' half-brother, Jude, had seen Him grow up with no sin. He'd witnessed miracles. He was there when they crucified Jesus. Then he saw the Lord face to face in His resurrected body. In Jude's tiny but powerful epistle, he warned us of troubles and false prophets that would relentlessly work to discourage our faith.

Then he concluded his letter with a remarkable promise: "To him who is able to keep you from falling and to present you before his glorious presence without fault and with *great joy*—to the only God our Savior be glory, majesty, power and authority, through Jesus Christ our Lord, before all ages, now and forevermore! Amen" (Jude 24–25, italics added).

We find more encouragement for joyful living in these words:

Listen, I tell you a mystery: We will not all sleep, but we will all be changed—in a flash, in the twinkling of an eye, at the last trumpet. For the trumpet will sound, the dead will be raised imperishable, and we will be changed. For the perishable must clothe itself with the imperishable, and the mortal with immortality. When the perishable has been clothed with the imperishable, and the mortal with immortality, then the saying that is written will come true: "Death has been swallowed up in victory."

> "Where, O death, is your victory?
> Where, O death, is your sting?"

The sting of death is sin, and the power of sin is the law. But thanks be to God! He gives us the victory through our Lord Jesus Christ." (1 Corinthians 15:51–57)

We serve a risen Savior, and we can bank our lives and our happiness on these three truths:

- *The Resurrection proves that Christ has power over sin and death.* So do we.

- *The Resurrection proves that the power to live victoriously really does exist.* We may feel spiritually and emotionally defeated at times, but those feelings are merely skirmishes. The war is already won!

- *The Resurrection proves that we have been given authority to walk in victory no matter what the circumstances of life.* Joy is ours today, fueled by a power greater than death itself.

The unbelieving world around you is without hope. And obviously, without joy. But you don't really live down here. You're just passing through. "If in this life only we have hope in Christ we are of all men most miserable" (1 Corinthians 15:19 KJV). But we do have hope beyond this life. We have it because of a Savior who walked out of His grave! For that reason alone, we ought to be, of all people, most celebrative!

## RICHES, RAGS, AND TRUE RICHES

I remember when my construction business was at its peak. Things were really going my way. I thought life couldn't be better. Money was coming in. I felt successful, and that momentum prompted me to build a very large and beautiful home for my family.

*I stood before the judge with stooped*
*shoulders and a heart that felt*
*like it weighed a ton.*

We planned to sell the house in three years so it wouldn't become a crutch to happiness, but I surely was enjoying it! When that house sold, we'd build a much smaller one, and the profits from the sale would provide college money for our children. The American dream, right?

As it so often does, the bubble burst. I related earlier how one bad break after another rocked me until I had lost everything. I found myself in bankruptcy court with a hundred other discouraged people. I had declared the type of bankruptcy where interest was forgiven, but every last penny of actual debt in my name was to be paid back. It was going to be a S-T-E-E-P uphill climb.

I stood before the judge with stooped shoulders and a heart that felt like it weighed a ton. "Mr. Crawshaw, you're not going to let this happen again, are you?" he said in a booming voice that all one hundred others, and the lawyers and creditors, heard distinctly. "Are you fully prepared to stay on schedule with this large commitment you've made to the people you owe?"

That was the most humiliated I'd ever been in my life.

As a former Christian financial instructor, I'd tumbled from lofty security to barely being able to pay the rent on a double-wide trailer. I can't put into words the devastation I felt. Negative thoughts hounded me day and night. Sleeplessness dogged me for weeks. I felt as if I were dragging a ball and chain, my own heavy heart. Often I'd go out and stare up at the heavens, trying to find the will and the words to talk to God. Small signs of healing appeared, but the weight still seemed to crush me.

Then one chilly night in the yard behind that trailer, shame washed over me. I don't know how low a person can get, but I was certainly headed that way. Humiliated. Broke. Afraid to see a creditor in public. Self-esteem barely holding at zero.

The stars were breathlessly magnificent that night. It seemed the fog that enveloped my mind suddenly cleared. I looked up, overwhelmed at what I saw, and said, "Lord, even though I am very discouraged at this moment, I know I have much to be thankful for. Not one material thing, not one piece of earthly security, not one point of pride from my former financial success matters in the least compared to the riches I have in You." I told you earlier about all the questions he asked in return.

Going from everything to nothing was a turning point in my life. I began to realize that joy and contentment are the true riches, and it's often difficult to taste them in the midst of too many earthly distractions. I was about to discover joy as a fuel to fire me through and above anything thrown my way in life.

Though I didn't just snap out of that joyless slump overnight, I slowly began to gather the heavenly manna of God's encouragement. The more I tasted it, the more I realized how much I'd been missing. God's manna didn't get better—it was already perfect! But I surely did! Slowly, I was climbing back into my heavenly seat.

A few months later, I taught a series of lessons on joy. Many people responded and asked for more. *Maybe I'm supposed to write a book on this stuff,* I thought. *I'm already an expert on failure; perhaps I'm supposed to tell folks about my struggles with discouragement as well.*

Remember what my wise old professor promised? "Before every blessing comes a test. The tougher the testing, the bigger the blessing." Mine was on the way.

## THE GOD OF *WHEN*

"Lord, how can I write a book about joy when my journey to joy is so up and down—two steps forward, one or two steps back? Am I off my rocker?"

I already knew the answer, but I needed to hear it. "Share out of your weakness," God said, "not your strength."

I was about halfway through the first rough draft when my health took a downturn. During that same period, my bills were running extra laps around my income. And, to top it off, I was really struggling career-wise.

"*When* my health improves, I'll get more positive," my emotional part said. "*When* the bills and the money even out some, I'll start living with a little more enthusiasm," my logical part said. "*When* I get some career encouragement, I'll start smiling more," my self-esteem said.

I walked into a drugstore one day with all that stuff heavy on my heart. I was writing a book about joy and struggling to get to first base with the how-to.

There were a couple of people in front of me at the checkout. I remember thinking, *When I finally get my errands done, I'll go to my office and look up some verses on joy—if this line ever moves!*

The little god of *when* was talking to me. *When* was smothering me. I was not only serving the god of *when* in my big problems but in my daily irritations as well. And it was about to bury me alive.

As I impatiently stood in the checkout line struggling with *when*, the guy in front of me was taking his time, joking with the cashier. *Why doesn't he just pay for his stuff and stop wasting my time?* I thought.

At that instant, the man turned sideways. He was having difficulty getting his wallet out of his shirt pocket. That's what he was laughing about. When he turned, I saw that he had no hands!

I don't know why he didn't have prosthetic hands. Perhaps he was being fitted for them. Perhaps he couldn't adjust. Perhaps he couldn't afford them. Or maybe he simply chose to adapt to the scenario he'd been given. But whatever life had hurled his way, none of it dampened his enthusiasm for living. He could laugh at himself, something few people can do.

He finally managed to slide his billfold out and drop it on the counter. Still laughing, he turned it sideways and, with effort, slid a five-dollar bill out. A dollar and some change were returned. With the nubs at the ends of his arms, he worked the dollar into his wallet, then somehow gripped it and maneuvered it back into his shirt pocket. With a big smile, he asked the cashier to put the change into the Cancer Society donation jar on the counter.

*Our eyes still glistening, we both smiled—
smiles that said,* We were blessed by
that man, weren't we?

By that time, tears were brimming in my eyes. He laughed again as he apologized to the cashier for taking so long. Thankfully, he didn't look my way, or he would have seen tears streaming down my face. I could see them in the cashier's eyes as well.

My tears weren't because I pitied him, but because his spirit rebuked my feeling sorry for myself. He had so much more reason to be bitter, yet *I* was the listless, ungrateful one.

I looked down while the girl rang up my purchases. As she handed me the receipt, I finally found the courage to look up. Our eyes still glistening, we both smiled—smiles that said, *We were blessed by that man, weren't we?*

He had laughed more standing there checking out than most people do in a week.

I walked out to my car and sat in silence for a long time. I asked the God of heaven and earth to put to flight the god of *when.* "Oh, Lord," I said, "You are the God of today. This is the day You have made. I *will* rejoice and be glad in it. I submit myself to You and, in the name of Jesus Christ, I resist the devil. I resist the god of *when.* In Your name and by Your blood, I cast down the negative imaginations stalking my mind. I choose joy. I come to Your throne to exchange the god of *when* for the joy of the Lord that is my strength *today.*"

> Though an army besiege me,
>     my heart will not fear;
> though war break out against me,
>     even then will I be confident.
>
> One thing I ask of the LORD,
>     this is what I seek:
> that I may dwell in the house of the LORD
>     all the days of my life,
> to gaze upon the beauty of the LORD
>     and to seek him in his temple.
> For in the day of trouble,
>     he will keep me safe in his dwelling;
> he will hide me in the shelter of his tabernacle
>     and set me high upon a rock.
> Then my head will be exalted

above the enemies who surround me;
at his tabernacle will I sacrifice with shouts of joy;
I will sing and make music to the LORD.

—Psalm 27:3–6

I spent an hour in desperate, honest conversation with the Lord before I turned the ignition key and headed to my office. The god of *when*—what an oppressive god. Maybe it's haunting you. Would you go back with me to my prayer a couple of paragraphs back and begin to fight the good fight of faith against the god of *when*? Pray that prayer as I did. Start doing battle against every thing and every thought that steals your joy.

*Choose joy!*

This book is but a tip of the iceberg of the rich biblical truth concerning joy. But this tip of the iceberg can help you! Begin claiming the absolute truth that your heavenly Father delights—yes, delights—in you! He's waiting for opportunities to bless you *every day*. His custom-designed program of joy is out of this world. Don't leave home without it.

*For here we do not have an enduring city,*
*but we are looking for the city*
*that is to come.*
*Through Jesus, therefore,*
*let us continually offer to God*
*a sacrifice of praise—*
*the fruit of lips that confess his name.*
*And do not forget to do good*
*and to share with others,*
*for with such sacrifices*
*God is pleased.*
*(Hebrews 13:14–16)*

# APPENDIX

# Twenty-Five Gifts of God

*T*hese are just a few of the gifts God bestowed on us when we trusted Jesus Christ as our Savior:

**Acceptance**      Romans 15:7; Hebrews 4:14–16

**Adoption**        Romans 8:13–18; Ephesians 1:5

**Association**     Romans 6:5–8; 8:34–39; 2 Corinthians 5:21; Colossians 2:12; Hebrews 7:25

**Blessing**        2 Corinthians 1:20; 1 Peter 3:9, 14

**Citizenship**     Luke 10:20; Ephesians 2:19; Philippians 3:20

**Cleansing**       1 Corinthians 6:11; Ephesians 5:25–27

**Completeness**    Philippians 1:6; Colossians 2:10; 1 John 3:3

**Deliverance**     John 3:18; 5:24

**Fellowship**      1 Corinthians 1:9; 1 John 1:3; Revelation 3:20

| | |
|---|---|
| Forgiveness | Ephesians 1:7; 4:32; Colossians 2:13, 3:13 |
| Freedom | Romans 7:6; Galatians 5:1 |
| Fruitfulness | Galatians 5:22; Ephesians 5:8–11; Colossians 1:10 |
| Glory | Romans 8:30; 9:23 |
| Hope | Romans 15:13; 2 Thessalonians 2:16 |
| Inheritance | Colossians 1:12; 3:23–24; Hebrews 9:15; 1 Peter 1:3–4 |
| Intimacy | Ephesians 2:13; James 4:8 |
| Justification | Romans 3:24–26; 4:25; 5:1; 8:33 |
| Position | John 14:20; Romans 8:29; 1 Peter 2:5; Revelation 1:6 |
| Provision | 1 Corinthians 10:13; Romans 8:32 |
| Reconciliation | 2 Corinthians 5:18–20; Colossians 1:19–20 |
| Redemption | Romans 3:24; Colossians 1:13–14 |
| Regeneration | 2 Corinthians 5:17; Galatians 6:15; Ephesians 2:10; Titus 3:5 |
| Relationship | John 1:12; 15:5; 1 Corinthians 3:9; Romans 7:4; 1 John 3:1–2 |
| Sanctification | John 17:17; 1 Corinthians 1:2; 6:11 |
| Security | John 10:29; Ephesians 1:13–14; 4:30 |

Moody Press, a ministry of Moody Bible Institute,
is designed for education, evangelization, and edification.
If we may assist you in knowing more about Christ
and the Christian life, please write us without obligation:
Moody Press, c/o MLM, Chicago, Illinois 60610.